P9-DMC-415

Mastery
And Management
of Time

Sydney F. Love

Prentice-Hall, Inc.

Englewood Cliffs, NJ

© 1978 SYDNEY F. LOVE

All rights reserved. No part of this book may be reproduced in any form or by any means, without permission in writing from the publisher.

Fifth Printing . . . . . January, 1981

Library of Congress Cataloging in Publication Data

Love, Sydney F.
    Mastery and management of time.

    1. Time allocation. I. Title.
HD38.L62   640   78-8229
ISBN 0-13-559971-7

Printed in the United States of America

HOW THIS BOOK WILL HELP YOU
MASTER YOUR TIME

This book shows you how to make effective and efficient use of your most precious non-renewable resource—time. You will learn how to direct your precious time capital toward the achievement of your purposes, whatever they may be. With the help of this book, you will be able to accomplish more than you ever imagined possible.

This Book Is Organized For Your Benefit

At the very beginning is the INSTANT LOCATOR OF TIME SAVING TIPS AND IDEAS. This is your key to immediate benefits from this book. Name your time problem, look it up in this special index, then go directly to the techniques and tips in the book that relate to your problem. Instantly, you'll have a solution!

Each chapter is built around a basic time principle which is explained and then illustrated by examples and case histories. This is followed by five to ten specific techniques of practical value for saving time on paperwork, meetings, problem solving and other specific day-to-day tasks. At the end of each chapter is a practical "Guide For Time Mastery." This action guide enables you to extend the principles again and again into the activities you are engaged in every day.

The first eight chapters deal with the basic principles of time management. When you complete this part of the book, you will know how to decide what you want to do, when you will do it, and how to do it efficiently. In the second, more advanced, part of the book, you will find seven more principles for accomplishing more in less time.

Chapter 1 asks "Have you got better things to do with your time?" If you have, then you must gain time on some of your activities by using the fundamental time tradeoff which is explained in the *Time Awareness Principle*. Because of this fundamental tradeoff, you can actually calculate the minimum monetary value of your time. This chapter also contains five ways to make the principle work for you in doing paperwork, telephoning and attending meetings. You are shown how to analyze and find out where your time is going. At the end of the chapter you start on the development of your own activity list for use in improving your time management. Each chapter contains such an activity list.

Reducing your work load is the subject of chapter 2. From the *Elimination Principle* you learn that there are three situations where it's simply not worth your time to do a task. You'll read about the manager who said "no" all the way to the top. You'll also find six time-saving ways to employ the *Elimination Principle*. For example, you are told of several ways to get that junk mail out of your line of action. For your own unique work load, you are given specific guidelines on what to do to cut out work that you need not do.

In chapter 3, you learn how to decide your time priorities. I explain how I've made good use of priority cards, and then show you how you can use a stack of small cards for sorting out your own priorities according to purpose. The chapter ends with a step-by-step procedure for establishing your priorities and shows how to keep them in front of you to master your time.

How to budget time and be in control of it is explained in chapter 4. You'll see how to get the most for the least when time is scarce. The basic principle in this chapter is the *Maximum Utility Principle*. Included are six specific techniques for using it in different kinds of work situations.

Shortening the time for the task is the objective of chapter 5 which deals with the *Alternative Principle*. You are shown exactly how to find alternative methods which take less time. In addition, there are eight tips on saving time when handling your mail; eight ways to save time with periodicals; and eight practical techniques to minimize time lost in meetings. The guidelines to time mastery at the end of the chapter show you how to go about developing your own alternative methods for saving time.

Chapter 6 shows how to do two things at once—a key to effective time management! When you understand the reasoning behind this chapter, you will gain a lot of time by using the *Addition Principle*. Also in this chapter is a list of 16 things you can do while engaged in very routine driving. There are five other time saving techniques—such as how to capitalize on the reading and listening speed difference. You are then shown how to use your activity list for finding opportunities to do two things at once—or maybe even three!

Chapter 7 tells how to make a single effort count for many uses. The *Multiplication Principle* is explained in practical, everyday terms. It is a real breakthrough in efficient time management. There are eight techniques in this chapter for applying the principle in your day-to-day affairs.

A little time invested in planning will pay a big time-dividend later on—as chapter 8 proves. You may invest time in training subordinates to take over some of your work, for example. You may also invest money in equipment which will allow you to do more in less time. This chapter even tells you how to cut down on repeated telephone interruptions by a small investment of time. It's all part of the *Investment Principle*. At the end of the chapter is a list of devices for extending your capacity to do more.

Time-saving methods for storing information are

explained in chapter 9. Here you'll find six smart ways to use the *Retrieval Principle*—in filing; in project workbooks; special reports; in giving special instructions; in agendas; and in minutes of meetings. All of these make use of the basic patterning of human memory which needs organized clues for fast retrieval.

If you're like most people, there are very probably times when you are overwhelmed with crises. Chapter 10 shows you how to handle these situations with the *Division Principle*. I tell you, for example, how this approach paid off in one of my jobs in a big way. There are times when you know that you can't get everything done.

How to separate the vital few activities from the trivial many is explained in chapter 11. I show you how to use the *Pareto Principle* in responding to daily priorities, returning telephone calls, and being selective about going to meetings. At the end of the chapter are some concrete things you can do for yourself to help manage your time.

The *Threshold and Saturation Principle* is explained in chapter 12. This chapter explains why, between the extremes of overdoing and underdoing a task, any additional effort is rewarded by additional accomplishment. In this chapter, you'll be given 11 specific ways to use this principle for accomplishing more in a given time.

Chapter 13 provides you with practical ways to increase your ability to accomplish more. You are shown how to identify the skills, know-how and basic knowledge that you need in order to get ahead by being able to accomplish more. The *Input-Output Principle* is a way to find out how you can increase your job accomplishment. There is a logical and practical way of going about improving your outputs and speeding up your inputs. For example, you are shown six ways to speed up your useful input from reading.

By using the *Revision Principle*—as explained in chapter 14—you will reduce the risk of expensive revision or outright failure on a new project. You will know the best strategy to get to a new goal when the route is uncharted. You'll find seven ways of making the Revision Principle save time for you. One of these is a list of phases to go through in rebuilding an organization—a "model" to follow in dealing with other tasks.

In chapter 15, you'll learn how the *Milestone Principle* will enable you to enjoy much of your work and be self-motivated instead of procrastinating. When you know where you want to go, and you are getting reinforcement from your progress, you can experience the sheer joy of accomplishment everyday. How to do this is explained in this final wrap-up chapter.

In the appendix, you'll find a checklist of time-saving equipment. With this list, you can plan to acquire the equipment and devices which will extend your capacity to accomplish more in less time. I've compiled this list from equipment I, and other time-conscious people, have used.

Sydney F. Love

INSTANT LOCATOR
OF TIME SAVING TIPS AND IDEAS

After you understand the time-mastery principles in the following chapters, you will be able to use this Instant Locator to solve your time-use problems. Simply look up the specific problem in the list below and go to the indicated chapter and page number. There you will find the help you need.

13. USING A TAPE RECORDER AND OTHER EQUIPMENT

14. DEVELOPING THE AVAILABLE HUMAN RESOURCES

18. KEEPING UP THE HOUSEHOLD

19. MISCELLANEOUS

Contents

A sense of the value of time. Benefits you will obtain from using the Time Awareness Principle. The Time Awareness Principle. Using the Time Awareness Principle in everyday life. 5 ways to make this principle work for you. Analyzing your time expenditure. How to accomplish more through Time Awareness. Guide to time mastery. What you should do today to start accomplishing more with your time. Time checklist for managers and executives.

Spinning his wheels. What this chapter will do for you. The Elimination Principle. Case history: The manager who said "No." Some reports and junk mail can be eliminated. The Elimination Principle as a means to reduce your workload. Guide to time mastery.

*Plan or dance. Benefits of using
the Purpose Principle. The Purpose Principle. How I use my
priorities card. Four good ways to
use the Purpose Principle in your
work. Making the Purpose Principle work for you. Guide to time
mastery.*

*Why you will gain from using the
Maximum Utility Principle. The
Maximum Utility Principle. Discover the advantage of budgeting
time. Six techniques for using the
Maximum Utility Principle. Obtaining the benefits of the
Maximum Utility Principle by
staying with it. Guide to time mastery. Checklist for mastering this
principle.*

*It's never too late to think of new
ways. How you will benefit from
using the Alternatives Principle.
The Alternatives Principle. How
you can save time driving to work.
Doing it the easy way. Six activities in which you can shorten the
time. Develop a conciousness of
alternatives. Guide to time mastery. Time checklist to master this
principle.*

Reading while listening is rude?
What you will gain from this
chapter. The Addition Principle.
Save time through these everyday
uses of the Addition Principle.
Five time saving techniques. To
save more time—follow through
with the Addition Principle. Time
checklist to master this principle.

Make one for me too. Save time
with the breakthrough in time
management. The Multiplication
Principle. How I used the Multip-
lication Principle in writing this
book. How Bernie R. multiplied
his selling efforts. Seven time sav-
ing ways to use the Multiplication
Principle. Zero in on this break-
through.

The rewards of carefull invest-
ment. Get time dividends from
using the Investment Principle
explained in this chapter. The In-
vestment Principle. How the Jones
used the Investment Principle in
the family business. Five tech-
niques for using the Investment
Principle on the job. What Norton
did to save time on weekly re

*ports. What Norton did to save
time on referable calls. Using the
Investment Principle to gain time.
Guide to time mastery.*

*Once filed, how do I find it? How
you will benefit from using the Retrieval Principle. The Retrieval
Principle. Everyday examples of
using the Retrieval Principle. Six
smart ways to use the Retrieval
Principle. How to get the payoff.
Guide to time mastery.*

*"But Boss, I just can't . . ." What
you will gain from reading this
chapter. The Division Principle. A
case history in which the Division
Principle paid off. Six ways you
can use the Division Principle
during "priorities pressure." Obtaining the benefits of the Division
Principle. Guide to the mastery of
time.*

*Too many calls to make. What you
will learn from this chapter. The
Pareto Principle. Case history:
Can we really please everybody?
Three ways you can use the Pareto
Principle. Obtaining the benefits
of using the Pareto Principle.
Guide to the mastery of time.*

Six steps to a lifetime of accomplishment. Obtaining the benefits of the Milestone Principle. Time mastery.

1 Using the Time Awareness Principle To Master Your Time

KEY IDEA
Not every task requires a high quality level. Time can be gained from one to apply to another.

I well remember the first time I actually kept a diary of where the time went. It surprised me and it surprised my fellow managers. We were responding to a request from our executive that we log up our time for a week and then compare notes. It was suggested that we list our major activities and make a note about every hour in a time diary. Some of the headings I used were: "Answering the Telephone," "Reviewing Routine Reports," "Shooting the Breeze," and "Miscellaneous." I added to the list as time went on because when I checked myself to find out what I was doing, I would sometimes identify a significant new activity.

The first surprise came to me on the matter of the telephone. Because of its ubiquitous way of interrupting my work, I had imagined that the telephone took about 25% of my time. The fact was that it took only 5%.

The second surprise came when we compared notes the

following week. I found that I was putting about three times as much time into correspondence than were my fellow managers. That gave me food for thought, and I decided to cool it a bit. Now that I think back, there was probably some private desire to achieve a writing career and I probably liked to see myself in print. Although this is appropriate now for my career as a consultant, it was not appropriate when I was a manager of engineering.

A SENSE OF THE VALUE OF TIME

Ron is a business associate of mine in Los Angeles who supplies office services to a number of associations. A few years ago I proposed to him a new kind of seminar which might not make much money in the beginning, but which had a great potential for development. Ron lacked enthusiasm for the project and when I pushed for a decision, this is what he said. "Syd, your idea sounds O.K. to me, but right now I have several other opportunities which have much more profit and excitement in them. Besides, since they're my ideas, I would much prefer to do them anyway. I've only got so much time to spread around on different projects and right now I've got better fish to fry. For example, I am behind on writing up minutes for association meetings for which they pay me $50 an hour. With a little effort I can line up more work like that and it will pay me much more than that seminar. Frankly Syd, I've got more valuable uses for my time right now."

"Well, I can see your point of view, Ron, and if it's not worth your time, it's probably not worth my time either. I'll look for something better to do with my time too."

Ron is a dedicated and hard-working businessman and he thrives on accomplishment. It just so happens that money is one of the measures that he gets on accomplishment. But there's more to it than that. He just doesn't take on any money job that comes along. He reserves his precious time for those things that serve his overall purposes best. He operates on the *Time Awareness Principle* which is de scribed in this chapter.

BENEFITS YOU WILL OBTAIN FROM USING THE TIME AWARENESS PRINCIPLE

When you understand and apply the Time Awareness Principle, you will be fully aware that your time is precious—for, like a moonbèam reflected in a cat's eye, it will soon be gone forever. Whenever there is something that you wish to accomplish—that is, whenever there is purpose—time has value to you because of an essential tradeoff.

Time is a non-renewable resource. We all get 24 hours a day of it. Some achieve things with their time and others get nothing for it. If you have no sense of time, then it merely floats by in an endless stream, like water down the Mississippi; you may lead a quiet and peaceful existence, but that is all. The joys of accomplishment and the joys of having a good time can be yours but you must first realize that time can only be spent once. Then you will want to spend it wisely.

BENEFITS OF THE TIME AWARENESS PRINCIPLE:

1. You will develop a sense of the importance of time and become aware of what you are doing with this scarce resource.

2. You will know how to avoid wasting time that can be better used elsewhere because you will understand the fundamental relationship of time to performance and cost.

3. You will know that your time has monetary value, and what price to put on it.

How to Obtain the Benefits

This chapter is an explanation of the Time Awareness Principle. Come back to the principle frequently and apply it to time-saving situations of your own. When you understand the principle thoroughly you too can become the inventor of time-saving techniques.

To help you understand the principle, there is an example from everyday life on how you can apply it to having your car washed, and another on arranging lunch. Then I'll show you six techniques managers and executives can use to employ the Time Awareness Principle. You will be shown how to find out where your time goes. You will see how the principle can be applied to: reading reports, varying the quality of letters, handling unwanted telephone calls, presenting at a meeting, and in other ways. Finally, I'll tell you what you can do today to use the Purpose Principle for the mastery of time.

Take a little time while reading this chapter to understand thoroughly the *fundamental tradeoff of time with performance and cost. It is the secret of good time management.* The tradeoff arises out of my scientific reasoning about the relationship of time to purpose. It is explained in everyman's language, and once you understand it, you will find the other principles in the book easy to understand and apply.

THE TIME AWARENESS PRINCIPLE

Time has value when there is a purpose. When there is a purpose, there is a fundamental tradeoff of performance, time and cost.

By *performance*, P, I mean the attributes of the new state of affairs brought about by an activity or task being done to serve some purpose. If your purpose is accomplished by the production of a new machine, then we may talk about its performance attributes or its results. If, on the other hand, the purpose is accomplished by participation in some experience, then performance will refer to the quality of the experience. In other words, if we are to accomplish our purpose, then some object or experience is produced. That object or experience has attributes which we can call the performance, although in some cases we may mean the performance level, or the results, or the accomplishment or the experience.

The *cost*, C, will mean any money which is employed to bring about the new state of affairs, such as money for materials, money to buy other persons' time, money for travel, and in some cases even the value of talent which could be used elsewhere. Our cost term might be looked upon as the sum total of the resources which are required to "put the show on the road," so to speak.

The *time*, T, is the number of hours or days or months actually devoted to the accomplishment of a specific activity or task. It is your personal possession of time that you may use effectively or wastefully.

If you work on tasks towards some purpose, then there will be some level of performance achieved, some cost or use of resources, and definitely some use of time. We are now ready for a concise statement of the principle.

THE TIME AWARENESS PRINCIPLE

> Given that the level of performance, P, and the amount of cost, C, remain within satisfactory limits, then time, T, can be traded off for either of these. If more time is put in, then cost may be less or performance may be higher. Less time can be used if you accept a lower level of performance or are prepared for higher cost.

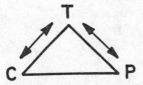

LOVE'S TRADEOFF RULE:

> Trade time for performance or cost on one task, and obtain more for that time by applying it to something of more utility. The performance and cost should remain within satisfactory limits.

Since time can be traded for the cost or resources and used in accomplishing something, then *time has actual monetary value.* The value of time to you will depend on how you can save money by using your time on various tasks which contribute to your purposes. The example below will clarify the meaning of this principle.

USING THE TIME AWARENESS PRINCIPLE IN EVERYDAY LIFE

Getting My Car Washed: A Tradeoff of Time for Quality or Money

Every once in a while I get the notion that my purposes would be better served by showing up at a client's place with a good clean car. In time-management terms, what I want to accomplish is the possession of a clean car. In plain words, the car needs a wash. This happened to me on a pleasant Saturday afternoon in May after several days of rain and muddy streets. I thought to myself, "I can wash my car myself, presumably at a very low cost, since I do have the resources of a hose and a brush. However, I'll need to use some of my time and there are better things that I could be doing. On the other hand, I might be able to cajole one of my sons into washing the car. But if I do I will have to fork out a substantial cash donation. Moreover, I probably won't be satisfied with the quality of the result because he will be in a hurry. Things were better when he had to borrow the car from me but now he has his own. Now it's an uphill battle to get mine cleaned because he's so busy polishing his own.

"Alternatively, I could drive my car down to a car wash and pay a dollar extra on my gas and have it washed in one of those 'quickies.' Still, it may not be so quick because it's a Saturday afternoon and there will be a big lineup of cars. Besides that, I would have to drive it there and back. Not only that but the car wash I would get from one of those roller brush machines is not of the best quality. The brushes disarrange my windshield washers, they bend my antenna, and the water leaks into my trunk."

I won't tell you what I actually did because that depended on other circumstances which don't enter into your situation. What you see here is that there are many ways to approach a car wash. However, given some kind of external circumstances, one of the three things—performance, P, time, T, or cost, C, will dominate. I might have been in a hurry and time dominated. Or I might have been short of pocket money and traded my time for money saved. If it was a weekday and the gas station was not busy, I may have traded off some money to save myself some time. In each case something would have dominated the situation and enabled me to decide what to do and what kind of tradeoff to take. Mind you, if I didn't have something better to do with my time, then time itself would not have been a factor. That is not the way it was. Time is always important to me because it's only here once.

Sometimes Time Dominates the Tradeoff

Let's take a look at another example of a situation in which you might get involved. Suppose you think about ways to accomplish the task of having your noon meal during a work day. You could go to a nice restaurant. In that case the performance or quality of the experience will dominate over the time and cost. We can write this P/TC. On the other hand, you might drive home for 25 cents and have a meal there, in which the cost dominates. You could write this as C/T with P not being important either way. Another possibility would be to bring your own lunch and eat it in your office. In this case it could be that both time and cost dominate the performance or quality of the experience. We can write this TC/P.

In a case where time alone dominated, you might order a snack sent up to your office—anything that's available. Then we could write T/CP. We have covered four ways for you to have a noon-day meal and each requires a different amount of time. What you choose to do will depend on the context and in all cases there will be some tradeoff of time with cost and performance.

Your Time has a Minimum Monetary Value

Consider the fact that when there is purpose, your time has some monetary value. For example, if it takes you 15 minutes to wash the car and you save $1, then maybe it's worth $4 an hour. In the noon meal case, if you get the same refreshing experience by having a meal at home as you do at a restaurant, and you can save $2 by taking an extra 20 minutes for a home lunch, then the time value would work out at $6 an hour. The value of your time depends on what you can trade it for in terms of resources; that is, what you can gain or keep from spending. In business they put it this way: The cost of doing one thing is equal to the profit that could have been gained from doing another. It is the "lost opportunity cost."

What is your time worth to your employer? If your salaried time is $15 an hour, it is actually costing your employer about $30 an hour, if the overhead is included. If you have opportunities to do moonlighting in your spare time, then you are not working on a fixed income and your other time has a minimum value—let's say, for example, $5 an hour. This is the value you would apply to your discretionary time, as you cannot charge yourself for time to eat meals, time to sleep, and time to make love. So the average person has at least 3 hours a day of discretionary time which should be given a monetary value if it could otherwise be put to earning or saving some money.

As for myself, I have put a flat rate of $20 an hour on my uncommitted time because that is its minimum economic value to me if I use it for teaching or writing. This means that I am prepared to spend money to be where the action is, and not waste time doing ordinary things or watching ordinary shows and movies. I will spend money to charter a yacht for a few days rather than spend weeks of leisure with nothing exciting to do. I try to do as many worthwhile and interesting things as I can in the time available to me, whether it be productive work, recreation, or mind relaxation.

5 WAYS TO MAKE THIS PRINCIPLE
WORK FOR YOU

1. *Reading Routine Reports: Some Activities Deserve More Time Than Others*

Take a look at some routine work you do, like checking daily time cards or daily progress reports. Are you getting good value for the time you devote to it? If you reduce the amount of time involved and just scan for major errors, will this be sufficient? If it is, then you can trade time for a small loss in performance and put that time to something of greater value. In other words, to save time on some routine task you ask yourself if you can reduce the time at some small loss of performance and then invest the time better elsewhere, instead of spending it on additional work of low value.

Here is how I reasoned it out with a sales manager at a workshop in Toronto: A routine sales report can seldom be done to perfection. No matter how often you check and review it, there will still be errors or improvements that can be made. In other words, the performance level of the completed task (the quality, reliability, etc.) is variable. Thus, if you accept that the performance is less than 100%, you can then accept 95% performance level and save about 50% of the time. The saved time can have more value if put into another activity—like selling!

2. *Relative Quality of Letters: Put Your Heroic Effort Where it Counts*

Let's examine an intermittent bit of work, such as writing non-routine letters. If you write a letter to a supplier to get some information on a new product, you can probably do a fast job because the supplier is going to fill your request whether your letter is great or not. You can trade time for performance.

If you have been asked to compose a letter for your president about a problem that you have been investigating, you will probably put quite a bit of time into it, and performance will dominate over time. **You are aware, though, that your time is important and you're going to put it on the important letters and cut it down on the less important ones.** Don't waste it on trivia! The benefit will be from switching your effort to the important things.

As a matter of fact, you could go one step further on the purchasing letter. You could circle a reader inquiry number on a card in a trade journal instead of sending a letter. If you have a secretary, you could just mark the magazine "write for info on this" and let her send a form letter. Looking again at the letter to the president, you may be short of the time you need to do an adequate job. Therefore you invest more resources in it, have a subordinate draft up what is required and you simply polish off the final copy.

Now you are being aware of time. You can gain time by using resources. You can gain time by dropping performance. Or both. Of course, if you have nothing else to do, then the time saved isn't worth a wooden nickel, but most managers and executives that I know are harried all the time. The nature of their work is so varied, however, that they are able to trade off time on one task to use on another, e.g., less time on a meeting and more on a new proposal.

3. Telephone Interruptions: Limiting the Effect on Your Time

Sure, the telephone interrupts you. You cannot be sure whether it is important or not. You can't live in suspense, so you answer it—thereby falling into the telephone company's sucker trap. They make you think it is a sin not to answer the telephone.

Many persons have solved this problem by having their calls screened. A call can be more important than what you are doing, but every once in a while a colleague gets through with a bag of wind. How do you get control of this time for your important work? Easy. Be frank and firm— unless you are prepared to give away the time forever in exchange for some hot air.

SIX WAYS TO LIMIT THE EFFECT OF UNWANTED TELEPHONE INTERRUPTIONS

1. Tell a long-winded caller that you are busy on some pressing work and that you will be able to call back later. Then call when he is about to leave his office for the day. The conversation will be short.

2. Ask your caller for an estimate of the time required. Then negotiate!

3. Steer your caller on to the problem you are working on. "By the way, George, have you any good ideas on how to . . ." You might get help, but the real name of the game is to get your caller hung up on something he really can't answer.

4. You give your secretary a signal to leave her desk and call you from another place. "Hold on there, George, I have a call on the other line and my secretary is away. Can I take it?"

5. If the call is through a switchboard, you can signal your secretary to arrange for a disconnect in the middle of your sentence. You can do this with an outside caller who can't clobber you—like the salesman who bluffed his way past your secretary's screening. You can do this in an emergency—once. After that your conscience will force you to use your talking skill instead.

6. You can read while you listen—a coward's way of minimizing the bruises to your time management by a wind-bag who should have his calls taped and played back to him!

4. Preparation of a Presentation: Using the Time Awareness Principle on Meetings

Let's look at a group activity. You have been asked to give a briefing at a meeting about your new project. **The higher the quality of the briefing, the more time or re-**

sources you must employ. If your boss and your boss's boss are going to be there at the briefing, then you will probably feel that: performance dominates over time, provided that the time for preparation remains reasonable. Cost also dominates time because we will imagine that your expense budget is really tight. You don't think that you can afford a full color video-tape production of your project to be made and presented at the briefing. Tough! No matter how good you want to be on the performance or time, there's always a tradeoff to be made. Right? In this case, you had better put extra time into making a good impression and take the time away from something that doesn't require top notch performance.

ANALYZING YOUR TIME EXPENDITURE

Many, many persons have reported that **they were surprised to find out where the time was actually going as compared with their perception of it**. Nothing speaks louder or more eloquently than hard facts. Try it.

You must make a determined effort to analyze where the time went as soon after something happens as you can. Take a sheet of paper and list upon it the kinds of things you do. After that, list some of the time-consuming ways of doing them. For example, you can list things such as communicating upwards, putting out brush fires, long-range planning, and chit-chat. You can also list ways of spending time on them, such as telephone time, correspondence time, writing reports, attending meetings, and so forth. After a few tries, you will develop a good framework for recording the actual use of your time, such as that shown in Figure 1. For each day, record in quarter hours where the significant time went. Record your time usage for at least a week. Add up the times in these activities and compare what you were *actually* doing with what you *should* have been doing.

What may surprise you is the amount of time that goes into what we call chit-chat, chewing the fat, or shooting the breeze. Chatting is inevitable and probably good for your

ACTIVITY / WAY	COMMUNICATING UPWARDS					LONG RANGE PLANNING					PUTTING OUT BRUSH FIRES					CHIT – CHAT				
	M	T	W	T	F	M	T	W	T	F	M	T	W	T	F	M	T	W	T	F
MEETINGS	1	0	0	1/2	1/4	0	2	1/2	0	1/4	3	1	4	2	3 1/4	1/2	0	1/4	1	0
CORRESPONDENCE																				
TELEPHONE CALLS																				
TOTALS																				

day of week

time spent to nearest 1/4 hour

Figure 1-1: Find Out Where Your Time is Going

occupation, but you can decide how much of your time should go into it. If you want to manage time, you must first find out where the time is going. Only then will you be able to take effective action.

HOW TO ACCOMPLISH MORE THROUGH TIME AWARENESS

Some of your time goes into work activities, a significant proportion goes into personal maintenance activities, and a portion goes into relaxation and pleasure. . Something which is easily confirmed by observation is that most managers and executives overlap their work time and personal time. For example, an executive may leave the office early for a game of golf and then spend two hours in the evening on some business correspondence. It appears to some that they are "workaholics"; that is, they work all the time. By and large most of them lead a balanced life, with accomplishment being the main goal. You will accomplish more if you use all of your 24 hours effectively.

You can take the Time Awareness Principle and extend it to activities and tasks on the personal side. You can take your routine tasks and classify them for the dominance of either performance, cost, or time. You can also take each intermittent task as it comes along and consider whether or not there is a dominance of one of these factors.

As you practice looking at your activities and tasks, you will become intensely aware of the value of time. You will think in advance along these lines: "How much of my time is it worth to put into this, giving consideration to the other valuable tradeoffs I can make with my time?"

GUIDE TO TIME MASTERY

THE TIME AWARENESS PRINCIPLE:

Given that the level of performance (P), and the amount of cost (C), are both within reasonable limits, then time (T), can be traded off for either of these. If more time is put into it then the cost may be less or the performance may be higher. Less time can be used if you accept a lower level of performance or are prepared to put in more resources (cost).

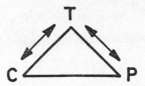

Main Points
1. Time is valuable because it is a tradeoff with cost.
2. Time gained by a tradeoff with performance or cost in one task may be better used on another task. (Otherwise part of it is "wasted.")
3. Routine tasks generally fall into patterns where either P, C, or T dominates.
4. Intermittent tasks will have a dominance of P, C, or T, depending on the situation.

WHAT YOU SHOULD DO TODAY TO START ACCOMPLISHING MORE WITH YOUR TIME

1. Identify three important tasks which were completed in the past week. For each of these, in the light of experience, which should have dominated—performance, cost, or time?
2. List three tasks which are ahead of you. Consider the situation and specify which will dominate—performance, cost, or time?
3. Can you save time in one of the above tasks by trading it with performance or cost and put the time to better use on one of the other tasks?
4. Calculate the average daily time spent on the maintenance task of eating. Now estimate the amount of time you spend keeping clean and sprucing up. Has performance, cost, or time been dominant in these activities? Do you wish to exchange

time between eating and keeping clean? Do you wish to save time on either and put it to use on work-related tasks?

5. Review the specific time mastery techniques in this chapter. Can they be modified for use in your particular work?

TIME CHECKLIST FOR MANAGERS AND EXECUTIVES

Make a checklist of your own activities and tasks on separate sheets of paper. The checklist below will help as a guide. Leave yourself room for additions later. Have it typed up and make 15 copies to be used with separate chapters of this book.

Activity or Task Descriptions (user to elaborate and enlarge the checklist)

Routine Tasks

MAIL:
- incoming first class
- incoming third class
- incoming subscribed journals for professional development
- incoming trade and business periodicals
- internal letters
- internal reports of peer operations
- daily, weekly, or monthly reports from subordinates
- periodic reports prepared for superiors
- periodic reports for peer operations

CORRESPONDENCE:
- replying to letters
- filing directions for letters
- proofreading typed letters

EXPENSES:
- preparing own expense account
- reviewing expense accounts of others
- administering petty cash fund

OTHER:
- regular local trips
- regular out-of-town trips
- regular telephone reporting

Intermittent Tasks

TELEPHONE:
- taking calls from superiors
- taking calls from peers
- taking calls from subordinates
- taking calls from outsiders
- returning telephone calls

HUMAN RESOURCES:
- recruiting interviews
- work performance reviews
- attending self-development seminars and courses
- resolving personality conflicts
- reprimands
- training of subordinates

OTHER:
- preparation for union negotiations
- special out-of-town trips
- replying to new and unusual letters
- special tasks for superiors
- listening to grapevine information
- unwanted chit-chat
- professional organization work
- reading grievance proceedings

Group Tasks

MEETINGS:
- regular meeting A
- regular meeting B
- regular meeting C
- high priority problem solving meetings
- monthly progress meeting which you call
- informal luncheon meetings

- association meetings
- appointment meetings

OTHER:

- group appraisal of potential recruits
- rehearsals of special presentations
- social activities of work group

Personal Tasks

- eating lunch on work days
- eating home meals
- preparation of home meals
- exercising
- getting ready for bed
- sleeping
- metal relaxation
- physical relaxation
- cleanliness of person
- buying, selecting, and changing clothing
- going to and from work
- professional organization activities
- self development
- reading of non-work nature
- watching TV
- going to the movies
- maintaining house and car
- gift buying and sending (esp. Christmas)
- socializing with work acquaintances
- socializing with family and personal friends
- major cleanups
- redecorating home
- correspondence
- watching sports
- participating in sports
- telephoning friends
- getting ready to go to work
- pet care (walking dog)
- transporting family members

Do This With Your Checklist

1. For each activity or task on your own prepared checklist, ask yourself, "Can I save time on this by trading time for performance or cost, and put it to better use elsewhere?" Mark as more time or less.

2. Identify those from which time can be borrowed and switched to those that would make better use of your time, in your opinion. Mark them for follow-up action.

2 | Tips on How to Reduce Your Work Load

KEY IDEA
Cut out work that no longer serves your purposes or is the responsibility of someone else—using the Elimination Principle.

SPINNING HIS WHEELS

It is 9 a.m. on a working day. Bill Brown, the vice president of marketing for a large soap manufacturer is busy doing some work from his in-basket. He is interrupted by his secretary, who tells him that the president wants to know if he can attend an urgent budget meeting at 2:30 this afternoon. This will conflict with his regular monthly meeting on the quality problems committee which starts at 2 p.m.

He decides to send a subordinate, George, in his place. He tells his secretary to see that George gets the file on the committee and the notification of the time and place. His secretary replies that George is out of town today and asks if there is someone else he wishes to send.

As Bill related it to me, his thoughts went something

39

like this. "If I send someone else, I need to take time out to explain what it's all about. On the other hand, if I stay away from the meeting, I probably will not be missed anyway because the new Quality Control Manager is investigating all quality problems and referring to me those which are my responsibility. Come to think of it, why should I attend any of these meetings? Originally, it was a necessary meeting, but three months ago we set up a new department with a manager to handle all quality problems. Why didn't I think of that before! The meeting is just a perfunctory review of what is happening to correct problems—and I already know about those that concern me."

Bill told his secretary to draft a letter to the effect that the new quality control manager refers all relevant quality problems to him. There was no longer any purpose to be served by his attendance at the monthly meetings of the Quality Problems Committee. He told her to telephone the chairman to say that he would not be able to attend this meeting because of the president's request and to follow up with the letter.

As this example shows, many persons are involved in **activities which no longer serve any purpose** with respect to their responsibilities. They are the creatures of habit and tend to keep driving hard even when the utility has diminished to absolute zero. Some things are best eliminated altogether.

WHAT THIS CHAPTER WILL DO FOR YOU

You can reduce your work load by first of all eliminating those activities which no longer contribute to your job responsibilities or to your own personal purposes. They may have value to someone, but they have no utility to you. Your time is valuable and you must be the master of how you use it.

In your experience, you may have taken over the work of another person and found that there were reams of files and reports that you never needed to refer to. The former person might be chagrined to see that you do not carry on certain activities that he considered important. Rest assured that *every person is doing something, sometime, that could be eliminated* without any loss of contribution to organizational purposes.

You are a creature of habit, and also may have an inclination to please others by filling a request even though it could be referred to another work unit. When you understand the Elimination Principle, you will periodically rout through all of your activities and rightly bury a few.

BENEFITS OF USING THE ELIMINATION PRINCIPLE ARE:

1. You will drop those activities which do not contribute to your share of organizational responsibilities.

2. You will periodically prune the tree of your activities so that you don't get lost in the branches.

3. You will have more time to do those things that really count.

In this chapter you will learn to employ the most successful tool of managers who were overloaded. Those who crossed the barrier into the zone of controlled time reported that a big step was *deciding what not to do.* So that you can intelligently lop off your overload, first learn about the Elimination Principle, then see how it helped Paul get to the top by saying "no" whenever he could. This is followed by six special applications for: reading reports; scanning junk mail; work of another's jurisdiction; unnecessary meetings; and office farewells.

In the GUIDE TO TIME MASTERY you are shown how to apply the Elimination Principle to your own personal workload—to the activities and tasks uniquely yours.

THE ELIMINATION PRINCIPLE

Activities which contribute nothing to your present or future purposes can be eliminated. They may appear to be your responsibilities; they may even come as requests for action by you—but when properly analyzed in relation to your work they have no utility. This is the meaning of the Elimination Principle.

Suppose that a piece of work has performance attributes (quality, results) when completed, which we shall call P. In order to get there it requires a contribution of time, T, and some resources with cost, C. We should consider whether or not the performance is worth the time and the resources required for it. A thing with wonderful performance may have no utility whatsoever in a given situation. Having a glass of salt water in the middle of the ocean would contribute zero utility. So would another seedling in a primeval forest. The performance itself may have utility in one situation, but be absolutely worthless in another. We can now make a statement of the principle.

THE ELIMINATION PRINCIPLE

> If the utility of the performance (quality, results) equals zero with respect to your purposes, then eliminate the activity or task.
>
> We can show this symbolically in the following triangle P, C and T. The time required, T, is set to zero when the utility of the performance, UP, would be zero. As a consequence, the cost is also zero.

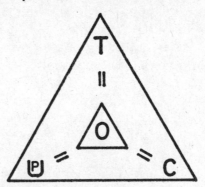

Let us examine how the Elimination Principle applies to several kinds of work in a general way. Later in this chapter you will be given specific applications.

Did you initiate the work? Work that you initiate yourself is probably important to your purposes. Delegation is more appropriate than elimination in this case.

Is the work your responsibility? When work is requested by another person or unit, it may have utility because it is your responsibility and it contributes to organizational purposes. However, some work requested by others may not earn you any "Brownie points" at all in your operation and so should be referred to another part of the organization.

Is there routine work that is no longer needed? Any regular work that you are responsible for is usually delegated, but the possibility exists that it has been delegated so well that you no longer monitor it. Subordinates do work because they are requested to do it and it is up to the manager to periodically check whether or not the work still has, utility.

Now, just one caution about applying the Elimination Principle. If an activity has very low utility it is a candidate for elimination, but it may also be a candidate for increased activity to bring it above a threshhold value to make it worthwhile. This aspect is to be covered in chapter 12.

CASE HISTORY: THE MANAGER WHO SAID "NO." (ALL THE WAY TO THE TOP.)

There were two top managers in a dry goods wholesale business in Montreal who were as different as a tomato and a potato. They had both been with the company since its founding and had grown up with it. Now they both held key positions.

Julian was the manager of finance and as such was responsible for all accounting, the invoicing, collections, payroll, and so forth. Julian had a nice disposition and was pleasant to deal with. He was liked by everyone in the organization. Julian's philosophy could be expressed as follows:

1. Always be willing to do any reasonable thing you are asked to do. If it's good for the company, it's important.

2. People will usually put up with a job that's done a bit late as long as it's done well.

3. If you try to please everyone, you will be well liked and will get ahead.

No one would doubt Julian's sincerity. If a customer was having trouble with delivery on an order, Julian would jump in and take action to please the customer. If he got a hot tip on a new business prospect from one of his friends, he would take time out to secure the business. Julian did these things in addition to his responsibilities as finance manager. These things were important.

If an employee's pay was to be boosted up, it would eventually get done and get done correctly. If a man's boss asked for it to be put through immediately, then Julian would endeavour to do so. Whenever anyone came to Julian with a problem, he would try and help them. If a customer was months late in paying a 30-day net account and gave Julian a good story, he was understanding about it. He did his best, even if the payroll was occasionally late and incomplete, and even if collections on accounts receivable were a bit late. You might say that Julian did his level best to please everyone—and if things didn't go perfectly, who would blame Julian for unforseen problems?

Paul was the manager of operations and was responsible for buying the materials and merchandise, keeping a good control on the inventory, making deliveries on time, keeping the facilities in good shape, and so forth. As I said, he was different from Julian. A potato is harder than a tomato and that is how Paul acted. His philosophy of work might be stated as follows:

1. Don't take on more than you can handle.

2. Say "no" with politeness and an explanation, but be firm.

3. A commitment that has been made is to be kept.

Paul stayed in his own bailiwick and did not mess around in financial matters, or in marketing or in personnel. When the work wasn't his responsibility he would weasel out of it neatly. Some people thought that Paul was just a little too obstinate. If he didn't have a truck available, he wouldn't promise a delivery. It made the sales people upset at times although they knew that once they had a promise from Paul, it would be kept. It was even rumoured that Paul occasionally said no to things the president wanted. If Paul wasn't the best liked guy, at least on one thing they all agreed—if you can get Paul to do it, it will get done.

It was interesting to see how these two executives progressed in this rapidly growing business. In 5 years the company had doubled its size and had taken on a lot more employees, including a few senior managers. The finance job became too big for Julian and he was demoted to his old job of supervisor of invoicing and collecting. Julian was given a manual of procedures and he only had to apply the rules. Under these conditions he did a good job and was even better liked than when he was one of the top managers.

Paul, the man who was ready to say "no" when he felt he should, was now the executive vice-president in charge of operations and sales. He was also being groomed by the president to take over his job when he retired in the near future.

In this case history, we see that some aspects of the Elimination Principle were applied by Paul and probably not by Julian. By avoiding work that was not his responsibility, Paul kept his work load down so that he could properly tend to his major responsibilities. He only said "no" when it was reasonable. He was avoiding the trap of saying "yes" just to be an agreeable person. He realized that he couldn't do everything so he eliminated those tasks and activities which did not contribute to his specific purposes in the organization.

SIX WAYS TO EMPLOY THE ELIMINATION PRINCIPLE

When applying the Elimination Principle, you should be aware that:
1. Any regular routine activity is subject to questioning as to its present relevance.

2. Any new request for your time should be evaluated against your purposes and present responsibilities.

3. You may indulge yourself by doing some tasks simply because you like doing them.

4. Taking on new activities just to be socially popular may not serve your purposes.

SOME REPORTS AND JUNK MAIL CAN BE ELIMINATED

1. Reports: To Read or Not to Read

Let us first look at a routine type of managerial work. You get *reports to read* for this or that committee or this or that activity and you daily take time to assess what they mean to your operation. After a while, you fail to notice that some reports do not galvanize you into action. They are read for information and then filed. As time goes on, you may only scan them, but somehow the activity is continued as it seems to serve some purpose.

There was a marketing manager in Detroit who asked for reports from the production department so that he would have a better idea of his future inventory of automobile components. At the time, there was a shortage of material and orders were piling up. He became quite interested in production processes and was able to juggle his demands occasionally to get faster response to some customers' orders. But business has its cycles and eventually the cycle went the other way. The inventory was enormous and sales were not nearly enough. Still the marketing manager continued to get the production reports and scan them because he was in the habit of it. Not only that, but he also had a secret desire to be a production manager—so perhaps he was indulging himself as well. One day, his secretary told him she needed another filing cabinet because the production reports took a lot of room. Suddenly, the marketing manager realized that the production reports didn't even have the value to him of the price of one additional file cabinet. **He told his secretary to get him off the list for the reports**, to discontinue the file, and throw out the old reports. He needed those production reports like a hiker needs a raincoat in his back-pack when desert hiking in the dry season.

For other time saving suggestions on reading reports, see the master index of time tips in this book.

2. Junk Mail: Surprises and Time Wasters

Managers and professionals are targets for all kinds of mail solicitations. Their names appear on dozens of mailing lists where they don't belong. They get elegant brochures. They get solicitations to buy this or that product; this or that property; and this or that subscription. There is no way to avoid being on these lists in the first place. If you have credit cards; if you are listed in directories; if you buy something by mail; or even if you only inquire about something by circling a reader card in a magazine; then you will be on a list which is not of your choosing.

Still, there are always interesting surprises in the junk mail, and so we scan it and perhaps waste a little time when something catches our eye. Among our third class mail are things we have asked for, and things that we are interested in, because of the nature of our business. We could eliminate all third class mail from our scanning and simply have it thrown in the "circular file" by our secretaries. This is one extreme application of the Elimination Principle.

A more practical solution is to adopt a routine with your secretary in which *she* sees that you are **removed from junk mail lists which are of no interest to you**. Otherwise, you will continue to get the materials. One must handle them as often as they come; they take a lot of space on your desk or in your waste basket. Nobody really benefits when you don't need it. The object of being removed from a mailing list is to cut down the size of your third class mail so that neither you nor your secretary are scanning more than you need to. Have a symbol agreed to by your secretary, such as RN for "remove name" and she will send out a form

letter with the mailing label stapled to it. In due course you
will receive less junk mail.

Assuming that your junk mail is under control, then
you have the choice of scanning all of your third class mail
or **delegating a pre-scanning task to your secretary**. For
example, she will know those mailings for which you have
requested the deletion of your name. Until implemented,
she can discard those for you. Then you can set down rule-
of-thumb guidelines so that anything that is clearly not of
interest to you can be pre-discarded. With a smaller pile to
scan, the payoff in pleasant surprises will be greater for
whatever amount of time you still put to it.

3. Say "No" to Work of Another's Jurisdiction

Let us look at the intermittent type of work which is not
as easily eliminated as routine work. A request to do work of
some kind usually involves a personality. When you turn
down the work you may offend that person. Still, the
thought here is *not to do work for which you are not responsible*, because that very same person may need you in some
other kind of work. To do work, or an activity, just to be
good friends, is not looking very far ahead.

The finance manager of a drug laboratory received a request from the production manager for a special study of inventory costs. If he did the job he pleased the production
manager, but got himself into some difficulty by looking at a
territory properly belonging to the marketing manager. As
well, the manufacturing unit had their own cost accountants and if the finance manager took it on there might be a
jurisdictional dispute. Besides, the finance manager got his
"Brownie points" by bringing out accurate monthly and annual statements. He was no longer responsible for any part
of the operations because he had been promoted to the
executive level. He therefore declined to take responsibility
for the study requested but offered to provide accounting
support to any study initiated jointly by the production
manager and the marketing manager. A short time later, the

matter was raised at an executive meeting and the company president realized that a separate operations research unit was needed to study widespread company operations. Had the finance manager taken on the study, the organization may not have taken steps to fill in a crack in its organizational mosaic.

4. The Unnecessary Meeting is an Unnecessary Pain

Now, let us look at a group activity. Meetings and more meetings are a heavy burden for the executive and manager. This group activity is essential to the smooth running of an organization but somehow seems to get out of hand. People complain that meetings are taking so much of their time that they can't get their regular work done. These meetings may have value, but are of no use to some of the persons asked to attend because of changes in organization, or because peripheral people are asked to sit in.

The problem for you is to keep meetings under control. There are those that you like to attend and there are those which you must attend, like it or not. If a meeting is of low priority but of some utility, you can delegate it to a subordinate. On the other hand, if the situation has changed so that it contributes no tangible output to you or your part of the organization, then it is time to call it quits. Eliminate it from your schedule.

A MEETING CHECKLIST

1. Is this meeting really necessary—for me?
2. Am I attending just because I like it?
3. Can I—should I—delegate it?
4. Has the original need for the meeting changed?

5. The Man Who Preferred Meetings

A scientific advisor in government was so well thought of that he became a member of many inter-governmental committees. The more exposure he got from these meetings, the more invitations he got to sit on other committees and councils. He enjoyed the sense of importance he obtained from attending these meetings and didn't question the validity of his being there. However, the time came when he was appointed to an important government executive position where he had the responsibility for the work of hundreds of other people. Unfortunately for him, he kept up his membership in the prestigious committees which now interfered with his ability to do his new job. His superior called him in and told him that although he had come to know of him through joint membership on committees, he considered that accomplishment on the new position was more important than being a member of prestigious intergovernmental committees. Besides, as an executive, he could now appoint a liaison to attend such functions. It was also suggested that he **drop his membership in those committees which didn't serve his present job responsibilities**. Having the job security of a government employee, he did not fully appreciate or accede to his superior's wishes and eventually was asked to look for a job somewhere else in the government. In this case, it is evident that his personal wish to be part of prestigious committees interfered with the real purposes of his position in the organization. He did not apply the Elimination Principle in the new context.

6. The Farewell Party

A colleague pokes his face into your office and says, "We're giving a farewell party for Joe. Would you like to be part of it?"

You think to yourself, "Joe? He works in another department, and he's really not an old work-buddy of mine." Then you continue the conversation. "When and where are you going to hold it?"

"Well, Joe is leaving for his new job with Apex on the weekend, so we're to hold a farewell party this Thursday. It's going to be at the Holiday Inn. The dinner and gift come to $15 a head."

You think to yourself, "These going away collections are getting out of hand. Besides, it seems strange that we have a party for a person who is leaving the company to work for a competitor, and nothing at all for the people who remain." Anyway, it's a social obligation and you can't eliminate the obligation completely, but might be able to *eliminate the time portion of it*. So you come back and say, "Look, that's the night I'm supposed to speak at my club's monthly meeting. Can I *skip the dinner and just put in $5 towards the gift?" You are settling the matter then and there, without further loss of time*. You are going to put your time to uses that serve your purposes!

THE ELIMINATION PRINCIPLE AS A MEANS TO REDUCE YOUR WORK LOAD

You can see from the examples above that your work context can change, so that what was once important is no longer important. You can be caught in the trap of doing things out of habit when there is no utility left. Likewise, requests for work or to attend meetings, can come your way when they properly belong to another part of the organization. These should be eliminated altogether. As the examples illustrate, not everyone eliminates a task or activity as rapidly as he could. It takes a conscious effort to examine the things you are doing, and it takes courage to eliminate them. Make the effort and apply the courage; then you will be managing your time more effectively and applying it to the things most useful to you.

GUIDE TO TIME MASTERY

THE ELIMINATION PRINCIPLE

> If the utility of the performance (quality, results) equals zero with respect to your purposes, then eliminate the activity or task.
>
> When the utility of the performance, UP, would be zero, the required time, T, is set to zero.

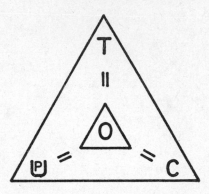

Main Points

1. An activity may no longer be needed.
2. A request for work which is not in your jurisdiction should be referred to its proper place.
3. You may serve another person's purposes better than your own by taking on a task simply because it attracts you.
4. It takes courage to eliminate a task brought on by social pressures.

What to Do for Your Own Unique Workload

1. Review your logbook or appointment book for the past month and mark *off those activities which were useless* insofar as your job purposes were concerned. Make a short list of repeated activities which have potential for elimination.

2. Make a list of those activities which are ahead of you for the next day, week or month. Are any of these *candidates for elimination* either now or later on? If some are found, follow through on their elimination. This will pay you dividends later on.

3. Seek out a subordinate or colleague who can be trusted to discuss your activities in confidence. Ask that person to make out *a list of the things they see you doing* and to suggest those which they think

might be eliminated. This list will help you perceive yourself as others perceive you.

There is another person who has a great interest in seeing you eliminate those things which are not paying off. That person is your boss (unless you are at the very top). If it is your good fortune to be able to *discuss your activities with your superior*, then do it.

4. When you have tidied your own workload, go to *work on that of your subordinates*. Ask them to make up lists of activities done by every person in their own bailiwick. This will bring out surprising things because deep in the organizational woodwork are termites eating away profits by doing things that should have been discontinued long ago. Because they were established by superiors, there is great reluctance to discontinue them.

Go Deeper with a Checklist

Refer to the time checklist at the end of chapter 1. Enlarge the checklist of routine tasks, intermittent tasks, group tasks and personal tasks to include specific ones of your own. (If you make 15 copies now you can use them with other chapters in this book.)

1. Mark the ones you think are candidates for elimination.
2. Make an action plan to eliminate part of your present workload.

3 | Mastering Your Time Priorities

KEY IDEA
If a task serves purposes, it has utility. If it has high utility, then give it high priority.

PLAN OR DANCE

"I have so much work to do that I just don't know where to begin." is the kind of statement made by many of the time-harried professionals I have talked to. They are very busy, but also confused. The work overwhelms them so much that they end up running from this task to that without any sense of order.

Compare the above statement with those made by other people I asked, "How to you organize your time?" Some of the answers are below. While they seem sensible, they nearly all have a flaw.

* "I do the urgent things first." (When everything is urgent then even an unproductive task may get done by the same rule.)
* "I do all the short tasks first." (Even the unimportant. ones?)

* "I do what the president wants first." (The boss-directed person is seldom high on initiative.)

* "I do things in the order that they arrive. First come, first served." (The last thing to arrive could be the most important.)

* "I set aside every morning for uninterrupted work. I usually do not schedule any appointments or go to any meetings in the morning and all telephone calls are screened. I work about two hours on correspondence and telephoning and then I take two hours for long-term planning work." (Top executives can do this. Subordinates must wait while the top banana does what he's supposed to be doing.)

* "I do whatever I'm pressured to do at the moment." (This is the person-of-the-moment manager who will forget about his president's request as soon as he is interrupted by his secretary in a discussion of typewriter maintenance.)

* "There is always a crisis to work on around here." (Management by crisis is all too common. Without planning— everything becomes a crisis!)

* "Everything I'm responsible for is delegated so I just do my professional reading until something unusual happens." (Superman planners are as rare as black pearls.)

Reactions to time pressures drive many people to strange behavior, as in some of the above instances. Some are working as methodically as a beaver building a dam and others are running around like a chicken on a hot stove. Some plan and some dance. In the instances above, people have a rule-of-thumb to guide them but they may not be accomplishing their purposes. This chapter will show you how to establish your priorities in the best way by using the Purpose Principle.

BENEFITS OF USING THE PURPOSE PRINCIPLE

All actions are for some purpose, whether they be in work or in play—so say the psychologists. The crux of the matter is being able to direct your activities to the purposes that count. Naturally, your work activities should be directed toward the organization's purposes. At the same time, you need to take account of personal plans. When career plans and organizational plans are in accord, there is common purpose. Even the Tuesday afternoon game of golf may contribute to the overall purposes by keeping you in good mental and physical health.

The purpose of this chapter is to enable you to establish a planning framework, which, if properly implemented, will result in a priority ranking of your activities. First, you will have the Purpose Principle explained, and made clear by the example of the priority cards I use myself; and by the example of how you would get organized to handle a messy situation like cleaning up the garage. This is followed by a method of applying the Purpose Principle in your work life—by sorting out priorities with cards. Other applications are to business trips and to meetings. At the end of the chapter is a section to help you master time in your own unique situation.

BENEFITS OF THE PURPOSE PRINCIPLE ARE:
1. You will direct yourself to high payoffs—priorities will be by purpose.
2. You will prevent most small problems from becoming large problems through neglect.
3. You will set an example of a consciousness of purpose so that your career image will be enhanced.

THE PURPOSE PRINCIPLE

Your time, T, can serve your purposes through the performance, P (quality, results), of an accomplished task. Your main purposes may range from the purely organizational to a blending of them with your career and personal purposes. When you know your main purposes, you can evaluate the relative utility, P, of a task with respect to the performance level to be achieved by doing it. The allocated time, T, will have more or less importance according to the purposes served.

As discussed in earlier chapters, all activites or tasks have the performance, cost and time attributes, P, C, T. All activities or tasks will require some cost of resources, C, and some time, T. Since our time is limited we want to assign it those activities with the highest utility. The utility, UP, is the value attached to the performance, P (or quality), of the task when completed. Utility from P is related to purpose, which may be monetary, psychological or sociological. No purpose, no utility. Known purpose means known utility. (A fuller explanation of utility is given in chapter 4.) We may now state the Purpose Principle:

THE PURPOSE PRINCIPLE

Given purpose, if there is to be high utility of the performance level of a task, then it is given a high priority on time.

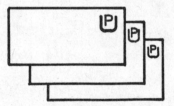

This principle does not mean that the amount of time allocated to the activity is proportional to the utility. Because cost and time are interrelated, you may get a very high utility from an activity by allocating other resources to it and using only a small proportion of your own time. On the other hand, when your time is the only resource that can be used, then *you put more time into those activities with a high utility* and less time into those with a low utility. This scheduling of your time is covered in the next chapter. However, some jobs can be managed well by carrying a priority card with you, as I show you next. As for purposes, I have assumed that the reader of this book is sufficiently clear on purposes to proceed with the principles herein. For those who want to examine their purposes in detail and polish them up, chapter 15 shows how.

LOVE'S PRIORITY RULE
IF A TASK HAS HIGH UTILITY WITH RESPECT TO PURPOSES, GIVE IT HIGH PRIORITY.

HOW I USE MY PRIORITIES CARD

As a consultant, I travel a lot. When working in a city away from my office I usually have dozens of things to do. My pocket diary keeps a record of my appointments and there is a small space there for reminding me of my major telephone calls and of things to do. However, I find this space inadequate for all the things that I do, so I carry a 3×5 card in my shirt pocket. It will hold about twenty tasks when written small.

On one side of the card I put the subtitles "DO" and "TELEPHONE" and on the other side "BUY" and "TAKE TO . . " I use a fine pointed pen and write small to get a lot on the card. Under "TELEPHONE" are the names and numbers of all those people I feel I should be calling from the city I'm in for the next few days. This is convenient, for whenever I get some time while waiting for a client, I borrow his telephone. The "DO" things are usually those which I do in my office or hotel room such as submitting a proposal, writing a promised article, mailing a promised brochure, etc. The "BUY" list is convenient because when I am downtown, I look at my list between visits to clients to see if there is something I need to buy. I also use it when I go to a shopping plaza, because I may have a half a dozen wants, and a memory jogger is just what I need. An example of my card in use is shown in Figure 3-1.

It gives me satisfaction to cross off the things I've done, and after a few days the card is mostly filled up with crossed-out tasks.

I found that just having a list was not adequate, because

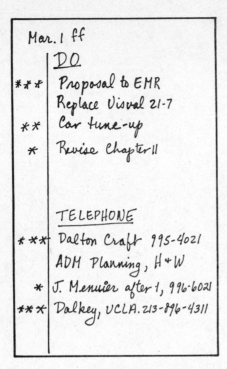

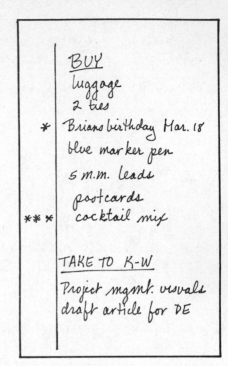

Figure 3-1: Example of Syd's 3×5
Priorities Card

when I scanned it down for the first thing to do, *I had to sort out the priorities each time I looked at it.* So now it is my practice to mark off the high priority items with three little stars, low priorities with one star; and those in doubt, two stars. They usually become three stars or one star at some point of reconsideration. I have found this to be very useful because there usually are more things to do than I can get done and this assures that I put my attention on the three star items which contribute most to my purposes.

To keep me in pursuit of my purposes, I carry a small colored card in the pocket of my address book. It contains my long-range purposes (objectives, goals). This is reviewed about once a month. My purposes do not change much but my focus on them gets sharpened up from time to time.

Even if you have a well-developed schedule in your office, a small card has the advantage that it is always with you and it can include non-work tasks as well. Thus, when you are leaving work, you can save yourself time and regret by reminding yourself that you promised your spouse you would pick up something at the store on the way home.

Cleaning Up the Garage Is Worse than Cleaning Up Your Desk

Let's look at another example of the Purpose Principle. Suppose it is Tuesday and you have an oddball holiday that cannot be combined with the weekend. You decide that this is the day to clean up the garage. It's a horrible mess. Your spouse has been at you about it. You can't get the car into the garage and you don't like leaving the garage door open to such a clutter. OK, you decide today is the day and you charge into the challenge. (A similar situation might exist if you decided to reorganize and tidy up your office.)

You well remember the first time you set out to clean the garage. That was several years ago. You were so full of determination you flew at the task, cutting a swath into the garage by moving everything out into the driveway. After 30 minutes you decided it was time to get rid of the small kiddie bike. You took it out and wheeled it down the street to one of your neighbors. He called you in for a drink and you jawed for an hour. To return the favor, he gave you one of his garden wheelbarrows which you could use for gardening. So far you were not winning but then you were not losing either. You got back into the garage and discovered your old manual lawnmower. Just a little oiling and tightening up and it was just what you needed for early Sunday morning mowing exercise with no noise or air pollution. You tried it out and found that it cut just fine. At that moment, you were signaled for lunch and took 20 minutes to wash up. In the afternoon, you found an old end table that just needed a little bit more refinishing, so you dug into that. At last the day ended; the garage had not been cleaned out; and that night it rained on top of everything left out in the driveway.

Now, you are smarter. With efficiency, *you approach the garage with a pad and pencil.* Lifting the door you notice that it needs repainting and jot it down. You also notice that the lock and hinges need oiling. Inside the garage, you see four bicycles. You make a note to give one away, sell one, and put the two others on a rack. This goes on until your pad is nearly full. *Then you start marking them low and high priority.* This brings up the question of how to decide what is low and high priority. You think *"What is my real purpose in cleaning up the garage?* I need a clean garage. Yes, but I think a higher priority is that I need space for the car. I also need room to store more stuff and I would like to have a clean garage as well as a safe garage." So much for purpose. You go back and mark high or low priorities on all of the items on the list.

Here is an example of what your list might look like:

Repaint garage door. (low priority because house needs painting too)
Oil lock and hinges. (low)
Sell bicycles. (low)
Give away bicycles. (high ***)
Racks for bicycles and ladders. (high because of space needed ***)
Oil lawnmower and snow removal equipment. (low)
Throw out old tires. (high, as today is garbage day ***)
Vacuum out corners. (high ***)
Shelf for cans of paint and car cleaning equipment. (low)
Go to store for shelves (high-low **)
Go to store for broom and dust pan. (high ***)
Throw out old paint. (high, as it's garbage day ****)
Paint floor. (low)

So you can see that *the activities are priority rated according to purpose.* A bike rack and a ladder rack come in for high three-star priority because they make room for the car and give additional storage. Painting the floor, although it would look nice, is low priority because it is barely seen from the street and does not increase the space one little bit. Priorities from purposes help you use your time effectively whether at home or at work. It is all from the same Purpose Principle.

FOUR GOOD WAYS TO USE THE PURPOSE PRINCIPLE IN YOUR WORK

1. Using Cards to Sort Out Priorities the Easy Way

Suppose your routine work is overwhelming you. These tasks which are repeated daily, weekly or monthly are consuming so much of your time that you have decided to do something about it. The routine work is not getting done well enough. You need some kind of plan. The first thing is to **list all the routine work on separate 3×5 filing cards**. List every repeatable item such as reading reports, making reports, reviewing work, etc. Use all the cards you want because they don't cost much. The advantage of using these cards will be apparent when you sort them into priorities. A list on a sheet of paper cannot be readily sorted and tends to force you into using the order in which it is written.

You will be surprised how the list grows. You may not complete it all at one sitting but you can always add additional cards as you discover more routine activites. Some big activities, like reading reports, require breaking down into specific reports to be read.

So much for the repeated tasks or routine activities of your job. Now set these aside and take more cards, possibly cards of a different color. **On these separate cards, write down the purposes of your routine work.** For a starter, you could look at what your contribution to your organization's objectives should be. For example, if you are a Finance Manager, one of your objectives (purposes) would be to provide timely monthly reports of actual expenditures. If you are the marketing manager, one of your objectives might be to contribute to profit by having adequate markup on sales. If your organization is managing by objectives, then you probably already have these in a desk drawer and you just need to jot them down on separate cards.

Now, there may be other reasons for your doing particular kinds of work. For example, you may have been requested by the higher echelon to do thus and so even though it's not in your objectives. You may have some career objectives which cause you to do work outside your general responsibilities just to please people, or to learn how to do things. It might also be that you have a special capability so that you are assigned a task which might otherwise go elsewhere in the organization. You also have personal purposes, such as playing golf regularly. Add all of these to your purposes.

Next, **go back to the pile of your routine activities and tasks. Sort them into three piles according to whether they contribute a high amount, medium amount or low amount to your purposes**. This is their utility. If you are doubtful, put them into a fourth pile until you can put them into high, medium or low brackets. One does not have to be too precise at this point. The main thing is to identify differences between high and low contributions to purpose (utility).

Now you are ready to look at the time required for each activity. In the pile marked high, all of them contribute significantly to your general purposes—but do they all take equal amounts of time? Not likely. Therefore, **sort this activity pile into two new piles by the amounts of time required, long or short**. Just leave them that way and do the same with the medium and low piles. They can then be laid out on your desk so that the activities taking the shortest amounts of time will be closest to you. See Figure 2. Look at the cards furthest from you—these are the ones you must improve upon. Some contribute high and others low to your general purposes. Those that contribute high to purposes and which take a long time might be reorganized so that they are delegated; more resources may be expended or the quality level changed so that your time contribution is less. **Those which have high utility and require the shortest time are definitely 3-star top priority. Those which contribute low to**

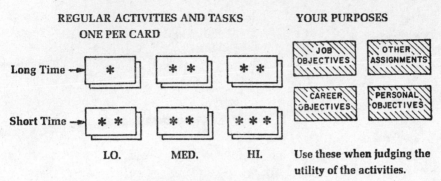

* * * 3-star, highest priority
  * * 2-star, medium priority
    * 1-star, low priority but not eliminated

Figure 3-2: The Easy Way to Sort out
Priorities by Cards

**purposes and take a large amount of time are candidates
for either elimination or a substantive reduction in the
amount of work involved. They are one-star priority at
best.** Times change and some things that were once important are no longer worth doing. On the other hand, there
may be things which are in limbo, so to speak, and you can
do them once over lightly and cut down on the amount of
time unless something unusual appears. For example,
scanning trade journals might be taking a considerable
amount of your time but contributing a small amount to
purposes. You could drop some of the journals you are
scanning, or you can have an assistant scan and report to
you about those considered important. When you are looking for specific information in trade journals, you can increase your scanning time to what it's worth to you.

You may want to try sorting out your purposes by importance. This could be a worthwhile exercise as some of
your purposes may be in conflict with one another. For
example, you may have a career objective of enormous

growth in sales but it could conflict with an organizational objective of high profit out of sales. (Woe to the marketing manager who hasn't solved this little problem.) When you get right down to it, a good look at purposes is necessary before you start ordering the priorities of your work.

When you are satisfied that your six piles of activity cards are as they should be, they will appear as in Figure 3-2. You can be sure that the highest priority (three-star) is the pile with high contribution to purposes with the short time; and the lowest priority (one-star) is the pile of low contribution to purposes with the long time. The others are all medium priority and those that you do will depend on other circumstances, such as your inclination at the moment.

2. Planning a Major Business Trip

Let us now look at an intermittent type of work and apply the Purpose Principle. You are planning a major business trip to an area where you have never been before—perhaps Central America. You will be thinking about when you will go, who you will see, what major cities you will visit, and possibly give a little thought as to what golf and fishing are available. You know that you want to see one or two persons in Mexico but you could use this opportunity to take a look at marketing in Guatemala and Panama. As you go deeper into preparation for the trip, you realize that you could benefit from talking to other people who have made similar trips to Mexico, and you make a note to do this. You find out from them that there are trade officials of your government in each of these countries who can help you to make contacts. When your spouse finds out about the trip, it is suggested that you make it during the winter months so that you could enjoy it together as part of a wedding anniversary celebration.

Whoa!, hold on there. Things are getting out of hand now. There are so many things to do that you had better get yourself organized. **Grab a packet of 3×5 cards. Start writing down the tasks.** Examples you might jot down are:

contact trade officials   talk to colleagues
get tickets   get shots
hotel reservations   get passports
car rentals   get luggage
make itineraries   insurance?
write letters   spouse or not?

Now you realize you have a lot of preparation to do in order to make a really successful trip. Some things can be done for you, but it is you who must make the final plan. If you could start on some of them now. Let's see. Getting tickets is mandatory and insurance is pretty important too. In fact, when you think of it, nearly everything is important; so that picking out the important tasks has not helped you order the priorities.

Now you think about the Purpose Principle. What is your purpose in making this trip? **You get out cards of a different color and you jot down: - Purpose:**
Meet your foreign representatives
Explore possibilities of increasing export market
Close multi-million dollar deal in Mexico City
Enjoy self
Come back in good health

Now it is evident that all of these things cannot be achieved with a limited amount of time so you **take your purpose cards and sort them by importance with respect to the company** which is going to pay for the trip. This puts a heavy emphasis on the business aspects and low emphasis on the pleasurable aspects. Now you can decide whether or not your spouse can go. If all the other things can be accomplished and you can add a few days of vacation, all well and good—but first, you are going to plan out the major tasks. Sort them out according to purposes. Closing that multi-million dollar deal puts the Mexican itinerary at the top. Add some details about having your lawyer prepare some documents. To get right down to it, if you can't close that deal then you are not going to make the trip. So, everything pivots around the major purpose of the trip. On the other hand, you might be able to combine some tasks—as will be indicated in a future chapter of this book on the Addition Principle. You might be able to use the Multiplication Principle too. Perhaps a game of golf is going to be your way of closing the deal.

Perhaps a side trip to Guatemala will have a bigger payoff if your agent and trade officials scout the territory first and then set up business conferences for you. So now you are planning because you are using the Purpose Principle. **When you are clear on the purposes, you can establish your priorities of preparation tasks and then you can actually make a schedule for the trip.**

3. Avoiding the Ego-Trip Meeting

Here is a technique for using the Purpose Principle with a group activity. Suppose your schedule is heavy and one of your colleagues has asked you to attend a meeting about a problem his department is having. Before agreeing to attend the meeting you ask: "What's the purpose of this meeting? Hmm . . . so that's what it's all about. What do you intend to accomplish? Hmm . . . well, I see. Well, I've delegated that matter to John and you will be better off if he attends. You can save us both time by calling John and telling him that I want him to attend."

What you are really thinking is that this is another grandstand-ego-trip meeting. John likes that kind of game but that you have better things to do with your time while your schedule is heavy.

4. Making Appointment Meetings Short

Many times an appointment in your office turns into a meeting. In fact, in some organizations, appointments are called meetings. Outsiders solicit your time through appointments. Persons reporting to you may need an appointment to discuss a problem. Sometimes, these appointments take considerable time and both parties are surprised at the length. Appointments lack the formality of a meeting and therefore an agenda is not prepared. Moreover, the closing time is not always stated because it is not known.

Some of the techniques for keeping appointments short revolve around having the other party stand; keeping them at the office door; having your secretary interrupt; and so forth. There is a better way of controlling the length of time required for an appointment meeting—apply the Purpose Principle.

When the greeting formalities are over, immediately **ask the other person: "What are your objectives for this meeting?"** This will draw out what the other party wants to achieve and gives you some idea of the time required. You take the time to say, **"My objectives of this meeting are . . "** **Then both parties know where they are heading** and should have a good idea of how long it will take to get there. In any case, the time will probably be shorter than if you skirt around the subject with small-talk about golf scores and families.

When both parties have stated their objectives, they have stated what they expect to be the result of the meeting. **Now you can state your time objective.** If it would take two hours to reach the objective, but you have only 30 minutes to spare; you can state your time limit and agree on how far you wish to go, or schedule another meeting. Perhaps everything can be compressed into the time available.

I have personally found this application of the Purpose Principle very helpful to the people I call on. I am usually the borrower of their time and I state what my purposes are and where I hope we will be when the meeting ends. My clients are usually delighted with this approach and frequently add objectives of their own which I did not think of beforehand.

MAKING THE PURPOSE PRINCIPLE WORK FOR YOU

Before establishing priorities and scheduling your time, which is an orderly way to do things, you must first think about general purposes. When you have these down on paper, then you can sharpen them up and put them in order of importance. You can then list all of the different activities that are commanding your time and put them on a priority card. You may also benefit from having a schedule which will have maximum utility for your purposes. (See chapter 4.) Not only that, you will adopt a consciousness of the Purpose Principle. When asked to take on an additional activity you will ask yourself: "*How does this contribute to my purposes?*" You will allocate your time according to its contribution to purposes. This is the Purpose Principle.

GUIDE TO TIME MASTERY

THE PURPOSE PRINCIPLE

Given purpose, if there is to be high utility of the performance level of a task, then it is given a high priority on time.

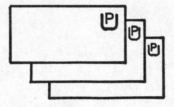

Main Points:
1. Give a high priority on time to those tasks which have high utility with respect to your purposes.
2. You can only establish time priorities when you have clarified your purposes.
3. Cards make it easy to sort out your priorities.
4. Your major purposes must be well served before you can modify the task to cover minor purposes too.

Applying the Purpose Principle

1. Many purposes of a job are implicit, that is, they are not written down. Make them explicit by writing down the purposes that guide you in your actions.

Be honest with yourself, because you are the only person who is going to see them.

2. Ask another person for his opinion on which purposes seem to be guiding your time emphasis— seeing your job through another's eyes can be informative.

3. Now for the hard part: What are your long-term career objectives? Are they consistent with your job purposes (or objectives)? If not, what are you going to do about your general time emphasis?

4. When you are sure what your job purposes are, put them on 3×5 cards and sort into their order of importance. You will then have a better mental model of your job purposes and it will help you assign priorities to tasks.

5. Refer to the checklist of activities and tasks in chapter 1. If you have not already copied these out on separate sheets and enlarged them with job-specific ones, do so. Fifteen copies can be made to use with this and other chapters. (If the checklist in chapter 1 is not for your kind of job, make up your own.)

6. Put all your recurring activities and tasks on 3×5 cards. Sort them into three piles of High, Medium and Low Utility with respect to your job purposes. (See technique in text of this chapter.) Divide each pile into two, for long or short times required for doing the activities or tasks.

7. Make up a priority card (or sheet) of the things you should be doing in the next period of one day to one week. Mark them with priority stars as shown in the text of this chapter.

8. Use the priority card idea for a month, making revisions to the scheme so that it fits your kind of job. At the end of the trial period, assess the usefulness of a priority card. Are you doing better with your time? Very likely! (It is possible that the detailed schedule shown in chapter 4 may suit you even better. It is a natural extension of the priority card idea.)

4 How to Budget And Control Your Time

KEY IDEA
When time is scarce control its use with a schedule—using the Maximum Utility Principle.

About a decade ago when I was a manager of engineering, my boss commented to me that he couldn't understand how I got so much done, not only at work but in my personal life as well. I told him that I did so many things because I wanted to do them. Now a decade later I can objectively look back and analyze the situation.

To start with, was I really busy? Yes, I probably was. My responsibility had just about doubled in terms of the number of people who reported to me. To my responsibilities for the design of television sets was added mechanical engineering, production engineering, and all aspects of engineering for electronic organs. As some of this was new to me, it required me to spend time learning about the technology and business of another whole product line with which I was not familiar. During this period I made regular business trips to Chicago and New York and also found time for a yearly three week tour of related industries in Europe.

Besides having a heavy load of business activities, I was active in professional associations. At that time I was the education chairman for a national association of managers, and chairman of the local branch of the Institute of Electrical and Electronic Engineers. As I recall it, I also taught one or two evening classes per week and attended a class in philosophy. There were other things, such as spending full weekends with my family, either going to a cottage or on canoe trips. Between suppertime and evening meetings I often spent time training my collie dogs and somehow or other I managed to do the maintenance work of a country home on ten acres of land.

How did I do all this? It was not as you might suppose, or as my boss supposed, because of a tremendous amount of energy. I was already in middle age and had no more energy available than most people of that age group. One thing is for certain: I had a schedule to budget my time from rising to retiring.

When I awoke in the morning, I would lie in bed for a few minutes to think ahead about the things I wanted to do that day. Then I would scan and revise the diary-sized schedule which I carried in my suit pocket. In this manner, I was able to get the important things done and not fritter away valuable time on things that I hadn't planned to do.

Objectively analyzing the situation now, I recognize that most people had diaries and appointment books—but **few that I knew scheduled all of their waking time. Therein lay the difference.** I can honestly look back and say that I was getting the maximum utility from my time. Aside from the recognition I got from my employer and my professional associations, I experienced the sheer joy of accomplishment!

WHY YOU WILL GAIN FROM USING THE
MAXIMUM UTILITY PRINCIPLE

Some people are masters of their own time—others are outer-directed, sort of like a scared rabbit in the middle of a busy freeway. If you want to accomplish more in less time then you must follow through from establishing activity priorities (chapter 3), to scheduling your time. If the time available to you is less than the total time required for all of the things you would like to do, as will be the case for most people who read this book, then *a schedule will be the best evidence that you are getting the most use from your time.* So that you will understand why a schedule is a good idea, the Maximum Utility Principle is explained next. Following this is an example of how John D. used one to prepare himself for his second job career. Then there's an example of how a one-shot project can be put on a tight schedule. In addition, you will be shown six techniques for using this principle. They are given for work situations where you will benefit from either a weekly, monthly, annual or special schedule.

THE BENEFITS OF USING THE MAXIMUM UTILITY PRINCIPLE ARE:

1. You will do those extra things which are close to your heart but tend to get crowded out by mandatory activities.
2. You will have a balanced program so that you will get satisfaction in many areas of your life.
3. You will obtain the maximum utility of your time, all things being considered.

THE MAXIMUM UTILITY PRINCIPLE

Utility is Different from the Dollar Value

One of the tenets of economic theory is that rational persons maximize their utilities. For example, automobiles may be on sale at the ridiculously low price of half their cost—a great value! One might be inclined to rush out and buy as many cars as possible. But suppose the possibility for resale doesn't exist. Prices everywhere are down. A person gets a high utility from the purchase of one car. The family gets additional utility from the purchase of two cars. Eventually, the point is reached where the utility of an additional car is practically zero, even though the value may be great.

According to economic theory, the rational person will then buy other things which have high utility.

For example, a person who has the wherewithal to buy five cars may decide to buy two cars, one power boat, one electronic organ, and a honeymoon tour around the world. If you can, imagine the situation in which a person has the money for five cars but is in a desert and desperate for water. That person would plunk down all of the money for just one glass of water. *It's utility that counts.*

This book is about the utility of time. The resource to be spent is a fixed amount of time. You can budget your use of time just as you can budget the use of a fixed amount of money. When you budget your fixed income of **money**, you want the maximum utility for it. When you budget your fixed income of **time**, you want the maximum utility for it.

Getting the Most Utility

In chapter 3, you learned how to employ the Purpose Principle by listing activities and tasks in order of importance. As it usually the case with the busy person, when all the activities that **must** be done are added to those that one **wants** to do, there is simply not enough time for all of them. Therefore, one must choose which ones are to be done within an allocated period of time. This is budgeting your time. You want to have a schedule that maximizes the utility that you get from use of your time.

To make a schedule, first block out time for those activities that are absolutely necessary. Put in mealtimes and prior commitments. Also allow some time for unplanned activities such as special telephone calls and minor problems. The remainder of the time is yours to budget carefully—usually more than half of your waking hours.

It makes sense to then schedule tasks which have high utility and require small amounts of time. Those high utility tasks which require large amounts of time are next if they cannot be done by someone else.

Using this reasoning, the activities and tasks that you

have identified in chapter 3 as having low utility and requiring much time, now become candidates for postponement. They can be lopped off your schedule until some slacker time—or they can be eliminated. A schedule which is developed by this reasoning will come close to the "ideal one" which has maximum utility for you.

THE MAXIMUM UTILITY PRINCIPLE

A schedule should contain as many as possible of those activities and tasks with high utility and low time requirement. Such a budget of time will come close to having the Maximum Utility with respect to your purposes.

⌐P⌐		⌐P⌐
⌐P⌐	⌐P⌐	⌐P⌐
⌐P⌐	⌐P⌐	⌐P⌐
	⌐P⌐	

**FROM THESE EXAMPLES, DISCOVER THE
ADVANTAGE OF BUDGETING TIME**

1. The Adult Education Plan for Getting Ahead
Deciding on a career change

John D. was in the dark. Not because he wanted to be, but because the electric power had gone off. The TV for once was quiet and the rest of the household was either out or sleeping. He had time for thoughts about himself. His working career was worrying him and without the TV as an escape from reality, his thoughts dwelt upon his career problem. For him to get ahead any further some serious re-education was necessary.

John reviewed his work career. He had started out well with a good education. He had advanced rapidly and had a comfortable living as a manager of accounting. Now, however, the future was not so bright. His working unit was going to be wiped out by the advent of new technology. Just as soon as the new computer was working he would be faced with starting at the bottom again. His present experience and education would be almost obsolete, and although he could continue working, he would take a substantial drop in pay. Moreover, the future didn't look very bright unless he could find a niche in the modern way of doing things. His plight was shared by many others in the organization, from machine operators to executives.

What he needed was some updating of his credentials and some special training in a new technology. It boiled down to going back to school. He could become a full-time student with government aid but he would take a drastic drop in income, and possibly he would lose his seniority in the company where he was working. Night school was the answer. Fortunately, it was still two years before the next big move. It seemed to him that the most feasible solution lay in some serious night-school study, leading to an updated diploma. Some of his co-workers had done this, and had been given preferential treatment in his company. If he had new knowledge, plus his considerable work experience, he too would become a candidate for rapid promotion in the organization to be built around the new technology.

Getting the time for updating credentials

Having decided that night school was for him, John faced up to the problem of where to get the time. He lit a candle and got out a scratch pad. On this he listed some of the activities which he would need time for every week.

work	attend night school
shopping	study
meals	society meetings
house care	club activities

car care   family time
entertainment   etc.
watch favorite TV programs

It seemed to John that even though he had purposes, there were more activities than he could manage in a normal week. He did not intend to give up working—or eating. His diploma course would require two evenings a week at school plus about two evenings of study. If he gave up societies, clubs and entertainment, he would have the evenings free but this didn't appeal to him. His chances for promotion at work depended upon the exposure he got in various organizations. Besides, he liked participating in them. He knew also that he could not become a hermit and give up all forms of social life and entertainment for two years or he would end up in the booby hatch.

John had learned to schedule his working time so he thought he would apply this principle to budgeting all of his time. Just then the lights came on and since the rest of the household was still quiet he turned off the squawking TV and got out a ruler and paper. He drew up a schedule for one week which included one column for every day and one line for every hour. Then he proceeded to block off some fixed activities. He knew he could manage on seven hours of sleep so he cut off the Sunday morning sleep-in. Then there were meals; work activities; a night a month with his professional society; and one night a week playing cards with a group he had known for years. He knew from a friend's experience that night school would be on Tuesday and Thursday evenings from 7 to 10 p.m.

John decided that family time would require special attention and could not be left to chance. For a starter he decided that he would take the family out for dinner on Tuesday evenings and they could drop him off at night school. Then on Sunday night there were his favorite TV programs which all of the family watched together so he blocked that out as "TV programs." He knew that if he got behind in his homework, he could use the TV time. There was flexibility in his schedule and it didn't look so ponderous after all. He thought it best to schedule study time for Wednesday evening and Saturday morning. He could use his office at work and not be disturbed there. That didn't leave very much free time for friends who would drop in, but one good thing was that he would be out studying in his office on Wednesday night when his mother-in-law usually visited. Now that he was on this education kick he could see some advantages to having a firm schedule. If this excuse would work with his mother-in-law then probably he could get out of that occasional Tuesday night poker game with the boys where he usually lost his shirt anyway.

You can see that **John organized his time** to accomplish a successful career change. With this plan and a reasonable effort, John was sure to make it.

2. *Putting a Project on a Tight Schedule*

Let us look at a time task which may require the scheduling of your time. Suppose you are lucky enough to come into a sum of money that will enable you to remodel your home (or your office, or your factory, or any unexpected project; we will use the home remodeling case to make a point). There is not so much money that you can give the whole job to a contractor, but it is ample if you handle the minor contracts and do some of the work yourself. There will even be money left over for some furniture. However, you want to have it finished before your folks come and visit. That is only three months away. So now you have a purpose. What are some of the activities? You make a list as follows:

enlarge living room window
replace bathtub
wall-to-wall carpet in bedrooms
refinish hall floor
repave driveway
take out dying maple tree

get quotes on kitchen remodeling
quotes on driveway
visit store to look at bathtubs
buy drapery material
make drapes
have carpenter build valance

You look at the list and decide there are quite a lot of things to do in the next three months. Most of these would make a mess of your house and you want it done and finished within three months or less. Certainly the driveway repaving can be postponed till fall, because it is more or less independent of the other tasks anyway.

You realize there are a few additional things, like repainting interior and exterior, so now you realize it's going to be a really tight schedule. You take a sheet of paper and turn it sideways and divide it into three spaces, one for each month. Then you divide each space into four for approximate weeks in each month. So now you have twelve spaces to write in. Bathtub replacement is urgent because the tub is rusty. You also need time to redecorate the bathroom. So in the first week you write: get quotes from two plumbers. In the fourth week you write: install tub, and the fifth and sixth weeks you write: redecorate the bathroom. Then you realize that the fourth week is your wedding anniversary so you turn your pencil over and erase the bathtub installation and redecorating of bathroom and move them forward one week.

Now, let's see. There is the matter of the wall-to-wall carpeting upstairs. That cannot be done until after the plumber is out, and it is probably a good idea to wait until all the painting is done upstairs. So you start by scheduling the painting and then the rug installation, keeping in mind your main purpose of having the house remodeled and ready within three months. You know you can do it but only if you have a schedule to work by.

The point I wish to make is that a special project can be done quickly when you plan and schedule it.

SIX TECHNIQUES FOR USING THE MAXIMUM UTILITY PRINCIPLE

1. Your Regular Schedule and How to Make it Work for You

Suppose you have sorted out the priorities of your regular routine work by means of 3×5 cards as shown in the previous chapter. If so, you now have a pile of activities which have high utility with respect to your purposes; or, by one means or another, you make a list of all of your regular activities. They are categorized as being of high, medium or low utility, and as long time or short time activities. You are satisfied with the indicators but you find that you still have more work to do than you can do in a given time.

The only thing left for you to do is to draw up a schedule of those with high utility and short time. You may need to ignore those with low utility and a long time requirement. If something is not going to be done, it had better not be something which contributes most to your purposes. That is why you need a schedule—to allocate your scarce time resource to the work with the highest utility. An example of a schedule is shown in Figure 4-1. The columns are the days and the rows are the hours in the days. Some people find it convenient to schedule all of their activities from rising to retiring.

First you block in those mandatory activities which you must schedule around. Do it with a red pencil. For example, during your work time there is the weekly progress meeting with your boss on Monday afternoon. Your own departmental weekly progress meeting is always held on Tuesday mornings and lasts all morning. You are pretty well committed to these.

Now start with the nitty gritty, that is, the real work that must be done. You *pick activities with high utility and low time requirement and make sure that these are on your schedule in prime time* so that you can do them well. For example, on the schedule in Figure 4-1, the weekly progress report has been scheduled for first thing Monday morning so that it can always be completed in time for the boss's meeting. When Monday is a holiday it can be rescheduled.

You could also *put in some of the activities that you do because you like them*, but be sure that these are in pencil so you can change them. For example, it is customary in many organizations for a manager to go to a luncheon on Friday with a number of his co-managers. This is generally encouraged and can easily take two hours. It is an option that you alone can evaluate with respect to your purposes.

THE MANAGEMENT OF TIME   ACCOMPLISHMENT SCHEDULE FOR WEEK Sept 20-26 FOR: John Doe 19---

TIME	MONDAY	TUESDAY	WEDNESDAY	THURSDAY	FRIDAY	SATURDAY	SUNDAY	NOTES
7 - 8								JACK'S
8 - 9								BIRTHDAY
9 - 10	DICTATE PROGRESS RPT.	MY REGULAR	G.W.		EXAMINE	COTTAGE		NEXT WEEK
10 - 11	GENERAL WORK (G.W.)	DEPT.			FINANCIAL STATEMENT	MAINTENANCE		
11 - 12		MEETING RETURN CALL			G.W.			
12 - 1	LUNCH	LUNCH	LUNCH	LUNCH	CO-MGR'S			
1 - 2		G.W.	INTERVIEW		LUNCHEON			
2 - 3	BOSS'S		APPLICANT		PERFORM-ANCE	WATER		
3 - 4	REGULAR				REVIEW OF M.S.	SKI	GOLF	
4 - 5	MEETING							
5 - 6		FAMILY	SUPPER	SUPPER				
6 - 7	SUPPER	DINE-OUT						
7 - 8					DRIVE TO COTTAGE	PARTY	DRIVE	
8 - 9	SOCIETY	NIGHT	STUDY IN				HOME	
9 - 10	MEETING	SCHOOL	OFFICE					
10 - 11								
11 - 12						!!		

Figure 4-1

You should not completely fill the schedule with your regular routine activities. There are going to be intermittent activities such as answering telephones and unscheduled meetings. These require some time. You can take an average amount of the time required and block off some time in every day for these. *Label these as general work (GW).* The remaining time on your schedule is yours to organize in a way that it contributes most to your purposes.

There is one trap in using a schedule. It should never become a fetish. *A schedule is a target and as such must be flexible.* You will find that a pencil is the best tool for making up a schedule because it erases easily. When interruptions cause you to miss doing an important piece of work, you can reschedule with a pencil.

SIX STEPS TO BUDGETING YOUR TIME WITH A SCHEDULE

1. Fill in the committed and mandatory activities, like eating, meetings, travelling to and from work, etc. with a red pencil.
2. Fill in other activities by their priorities. Put those with a high utility and low time requirement into your "prime" time.
3. Put in some "want to" items to make your life more interesting.
4. Leave some free time for general work, emergencies and changes in priorities.
5. The time targets should be reasonable so that you can usually achieve them.
6. Be flexible. Replan when circumstances change.

2. A Tip on Using Your Appointment Book as a Schedule

A managerial colleague of mine complained that he simply could not plan his time. There were too many crises and too many demands for his time which could not be planned in advance. "OK," I said, "You do it your way and I'll do it mine—by the way, can you give me an appointment for Tuesday from two to three o'clock to discuss our managerial exchange training plan? I have two junior managers who want to work in your department."

Unaware of my game, he replied something like: "Sure, just let me check my appointment book. Oh yes, two o'clock it is. I'll be here in my office for sure."

"Just out of curiosity—do you always keep an appointment?"

"Certainly. I make every effort to do so, and if something does interfere with it I get my secretary to call and arrange another time. After all, we must be organized."

"Well, why don't you make appointments with yourself to do some of the work that you find so hard to schedule." I said. Then he grinned as he got the message.

My friend found that he could **make appointments with himself** much more easily than he could make an overall schedule for the week (see Figure 4-2). His dedication to

Fig. 4-2: An Appointment with One's Self
is a Way to Schedule

keeping appointments was fanatical and was put to work as a planning motivator. After a while his appointment book had to be enlarged because he was scheduling a lot of his own time in it.

An appointment book is not to be confused with a schedule. An appointment book is useful for your secretary to give appointments within blocks of time that you have allocated to general work. A schedule, on the other hand, usually requires a lot more space and can benefit from the use of colored pencils as well. Moreover, a schedule is something that you want at your desk so that you can refer to it frequently. Your secretary should transfer appointments from the appointment book to your schedule. On the other hand, if you do dispense with the appointment book, simply have a stack of weekly schedules stapled together and use those for appointments as well as for scheduling

3. Zeroing In on a Schedule for a Special Business Trip

Suppose you are planning a special business trip to Central America. You have made the final arrangements to close a multi-million dollar business deal in Mexico City and the date has been set. You are now ready to schedule those dozen or so activities that lead up to and surround this major business trip. You take out some scratch paper and *rough out a four-month schedule with lines for every week.* You then give it to your secretary to redraw and then indicate on it the major commitments of time that you have. You also ask her to rough in a schedule for the routine trip activities, such as obtaining a passport. You also dictate a list of all the activities that you want to plan to do and ask her to type them one after the other on a sheet of paper with two carbon copies.

You make a note on your regular schedule to *work on this special plan* tomorrow morning because your vacation is coming up and you want to get some things under way beforehand.

Routine business trips can go on your regular weekly

schedule but **when a special trip requires long-term planning, you will do better by making a special schedule to suit the planning time frame.**

4. *The Man Who Scheduled Everything but Used a Hot-Line to Override It*

A friend of mine, an immigrant from Germany, took scheduling so seriously that he carried it to extremes. He even scheduled his telephone calls from me. "Call me at 3 p.m. on Tuesday and I'll give you the answer."

So I called him at 3 p.m. on Tuesday and found that the line was busy. With the use of my repertory dialer which electronically remembered his number, I conveniently dialed his number every five minutes for 30 minutes. On my seventh try I got through, only to find out that he had just left his office to attend a meeting. You see, the scheduling of his telephone calls worked very well for him, but it didn't work so well for me.

When I checked with him a month later he was still certain that he could schedule telephone calls. For example, he told me that he had educated most of his subordinates to telephone him after 4 p.m. unless it was extremely urgent. He had tried to schedule the president's calls, but failing in this, he went to the other extreme and had a *special telephone installed with an unlisted number. He called it his* "hot line". So I noticed that even he found out that not everything could be scheduled. To this day I am wondering whether or not he tried to schedule his sex life. I suppose it depended on who had the number to his "hot line."

5. *The One-Year Conference Schedule*

A science advisor in government was required to be up to date in his field and to establish world-wide contacts. He attended an unusually large number of international conferences and seminars. On the wall of his office he had *two one-year planning charts* for which there was a box for every week in the year. On it he had scheduled conferences with notations at the end for those conferences in the following years.

As time went on he found more uses for his one-year planning chart, although the nature of his work was such that he did not require a detailed weekly schedule. He added notations about major monthly meetings, scheduled annual reviews and special reports.

You see, not everyone needs a weekly schedule, or even a monthly one. **Your schedule time frame depends on the kind of job you do**.

6. Team Scheduling for a Project

CPM/PERT is an advanced technique for planning and scheduling many activities. The following example shows how it works.

A task force was assembled for a special project— moving the headquarters office of a Chicago insurance firm to a new site. Henry J. was selected to be the project leader in charge of the task force. The preseident knew that in order for the change to be effected on schedule, the project leader needed a bit of clout. He arranged for Henry to report to him directly about this specific task. For his regular work Henry reported to a much lower level. The president also gave the project leader the authority to communicate up and down and across the organization, wherever the task required it, without regard to the usual channels. Just for good measure, the president sent Henry to a seminar on project management techniques.

Henry returned from the seminar all charged up with new ideas which he immediately started to put in place. He started with the CPM/PERT technique of planning, scheduling and controlling. The subtasks were listed and the precedence relations worked out. For example, agreements needed to be reached on how much space would be allocated to each department before the architects could go ahead with their plans; a decision had to be reached on whether to use an expensive energy conservation technique before the contracts were let; new arrangements had to be made for a centralized telephone answering service; the re-shuffling of responsibilities needed to be settled in advance of the move or the centrex telephone systems could not be installed economically.

Because the precedence relations for the CPM/PERT system required the listing of all the sub-tasks, the consulta-tive process was started early. All those affected by the move were required to give estimates of cost and time and thereby were involved in the planning process. Many sub-problems were ironed out before the move.

After the move the president commented that this was about the smoothest moving operation that he had ever ex-perienced. He personally commended Henry and suggested to his executive committee that Henry's expertise in project management techniques be applied to other special under-takings in their business.

As you can see from the case history above, project management with CPM/PERT scheduling is a good way to put a complex project through an organization. Dig into it when you get a tough project assigned to you.

OBTAINING THE BENEFITS OF THE MAXIMUM UTILITY PRINCIPLE BY STAYING WITH IT

As indicated in the examples above, activities can be scheduled for most occupations. Moreover, scheduling can be usefully extended to include all of your waking time. When you schedule your time according to purposes, then you will maximize the utility of your time. Scheduling is easy to begin but often a little hard to stay with long enough to make it your tool. One needs practice in making and using schedules. You can over-schedule and it can become a ball and chain rather than a tool to help you do the things you really want to do.

You need to find out which type of schedule suits your

purposes best. There are daily, weekly, monthly and yearly schedules to be considered, individually or in combination.

Scheduling your time is budgeting your time. You budget when resources are limited and you want to get the most out of them. It takes a little time to plan and schedule and for many people this is the big drawback. On the other hand, if you **stick with scheduling long enough to see what it will do for you,** you will probably end up making use of the Maximum Utility Principle. When you do, you will have a balanced program of activities that guides you into doing all of the things that you need to do to accomplish your purposes. When you have a balanced program, you will be well satisfied with your accomplishment and get that extra something out of life.

GUIDE TO TIME MASTERY

THE MAXIMUM UTILITY PRINCIPLE

A schedule should contain as many as possible of those activities and tasks with high utility and low time requirements. Such a budget of time will come close to having the Maximum Utility with respect to your purposes.

⌐P⌐		⌐P⌐
⌐P⌐	⌐P⌐	⌐P⌐
⌐P⌐	⌐P⌐	⌐P⌐
	⌐P⌐	

Main Points
1. A schedule is to budget your scarce time resource so that you get maximum utility for your time.

2. Activities with high utility and a low time requirement have priority on a schedule.

3. A schedule helps you achieve a balanced program.

4. You can combine work time and personal time on one schedule.

When to Apply the Maximum Utility Principle

1. Is the time you have available less than you need for the things you want to do?

2. If yes, then go on. If no, you are either well planned or bored to death.

3. Would weekly, monthly or yearly schedules apply to your kind of work?

CHECKLIST FOR MASTERING THIS PRINCIPLE

1. Refer to the checklist in chapter 1. Make your own list of job-specific activities and tasks. For each one make a notation: yes, if you think it can be scheduled; and no, if you think it cannot.

2. Draw up a schedule something like Figure 4-2 and make yourself a weekly (monthly or yearly) schedule. Be sure to allow adequate time for un-planned activities. Use it for one week and mark off the activities acomplished with a green pencil. If you have difficulty in keeping to the plan, don't worry—replan as often as necessary. Do this for at least four weeks before deciding whether it is for you or not.

3. Make up a schedule for a longer time span than you did above, e.g., if you did a weekly one, try a monthly one. Repeat at least once, and decide if it is worth continuing for your purposes.

4. When you have mastered scheduling for yourself, pass on this useful technique to your subordinates, and guide them accordingly.

5

Using the Alternatives Principle to Shorten The Time for the Task

KEY IDEA
To save time on repeated activities, look for alternative procedures that are better—using the Alternatives Principle.

IT'S NEVER TOO LATE TO THINK OF NEW WAYS

The financial comptroller of one of my clients delegated some work which started out as small tasks. It had gradually grown into regular work which could be delegated. A week later the delegate, Jack, came back and proposed a new way of going about the work. *With a slight change in procedure the work could be cut in half!*

In discussing this event with me, the comptroller said that he could have kicked himself for not thinking of the new procedure himself. He was not worried about what Jack thought of him. He had selected Jack in the first place because he was bright and had an elastic mind. "It's what I think of myself that worries me. Have I been on this job too long? Am I getting stale in my thinking?"

The substance of my reply was that not looking for alternative ways of doing a task is commonplace among old and young alike. Society puts such a premium on fast results that we jump into a task and try to show some results as quickly as possible. It takes a conscious effort to hold back and consider alternative procedures for getting the work done. It's a state of mind, and age has nothing to do with it—except that the longer we operate in society the more we can be affected by it. Young and old alike must take steps to free their minds from habitual thinking, and to consciously stretch their minds. Elasticity of mind can be turned on and off at will. One is never too old or too young to be creative. There are always alternative ways of doing a specific job. Some of these are ways which save time without impairing the quality of the work or increasing the resources required.

Later on the comptroller participated in one of my problem-solving seminars. He told me afterwards: "It was not until others in the group started calling out additional solutions that I realized I usually got stuck on the first thing that came to my mind. Now I always force myself to think of at least three ways to do a task before going ahead."

As a result of this man's discovery about himself, he practiced looking for alternatives. In two years he cut the cost of his firm's financial record-keeping by 25% and was promoted to the executive suite.

HOW YOU WILL BENEFIT FROM USING THE ALTERNATIVES PRINCIPLE

Many managers and executives rush into a new task with an enthusiasm that covers their lack of preparation. Like plunging into the bush, the going may be easy or it may get rough. You can have a clear path or you can run into unmapped swamps and deadfalls. A little thought about alternative routes will go a long way to reducing the time taken. This applies to many tasks, particularly to new ones.

Sometimes you will find that regular work is like a

winding road that started out as a trail in the bush. It evolved slowly and conveniently—with many wasteful detours. Now it's time to cut through with an expressway. In this chapter, we are dealing with efficient ways to use time.

BENEFITS FROM USING THE ALTERNATIVES PRINCIPLE

1. You will find ways to save time on routine tasks.
2. You will consciously look for alternative ways to do new tasks in less time.
3. You will demonstrate an elasticity of mind for problem solving.

To gain these benefits, first read over the principle and the example of driving to work. When you understand the principle, consider the six specific ways to apply the Alternatives Principle to your work. They can save you time. There follow alternative ways to read your mail, mine the periodicals, deal with a problem employee, handle a jurisdictional grievance, prepare and give a presentation, avoid wasting time at ad hoc committee meetings. After this is a section to help you personally to develop a flexible mind, and benefit from continuous use of the Alternatives Principle.

THE ALTERNATIVES PRINCIPLE

There Is Always Another Way

There are always alternative ways to do a task because of the essential tradeoff between performance, P, cost of resources, C, and the time taken, T.

Suppose you start on a task which is part of your regular routine. You can estimate the usual time but your objective is to find a new time which is less. If you are prepared to lower the performance level of the completed task then it can be done in less time. This is one of the tradeoffs wherein T is preferred over P. If you are prepared to invest more human resources or spend more money for equipment or contracted work, then you may achieve the original level of performance with less of your time. This is the tradeoff of time with cost wherein T is preferred over C. You may also reduce the time by dropping the performance a little and increasing the cost a little, both together. Then T is preferred to both P and C.

Part of your responsibility is to make decisions about the relative levels of performance, cost and time for new tasks or routine work. Because of the essential tradeoff of P, C and T, there are *always* alternative ways to do a task, even without creating a new and better procedure.

There Are Often Procedures that Are Better

Now let's look at another point of view of the Alternatives Principle. Given a bit of routine work, the procedure for doing it may be **creatively** changed with a consequential reduction in time and no change in the performance level. In order to win in this move, one must invest a little time or other resources in studying the procedure which is currently being used. Naturally, the big payoff on the investment will be in routine work which is repeated many times. A whole science of methods study has grown up around this concept. You get the same result with an easier method.

On a short task it is hardly worth the bother to look for alternative ways because you can get it done faster than you can plan. On the other hand, **there is hardly a task for which a 10 % allocation of time to planning would not be beneficial.** This is a good rule of thumb because even if you do not discover a better procedure, you can still get 90% of the task done with the remaining time.

Any improvement of procedure is really an extension of the principle stated above. In this case we wish to keep P constant and reduce T. We are prepared to invest some resources in studying procedures or in purchasing better equipment in order to reduce the time taken for a repeated activity. We are now able to make a statement about the Alternatives Principle.

THE ALTERNATIVES PRINCIPLE

There are always alternative ways to shorten the time for a task. They are: by lowering the level of performance; by investing more human or material resources; by creating a new procedure.

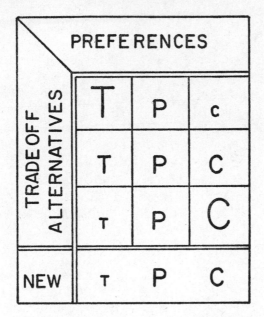

HOW YOU CAN SAVE TIME IN DRIVING TO WORK

That Long Drive to Work

Let us consider a routine activity which is quite time consuming for most persons—driving to work.

What follows happened once to me and I ask you to imagine that it is happening to you. One morning you are rolling along to work on the usual route. You know it so well you could drive it in your sleep. You find yourself slowing up in a lineup of cars at a detour sign. You are shunted off to side streets and see yourself being late for your meeting despite your careful plans to arrive on time. In desperation, you break out of the detour and run off into an unknown side street. After a few stop signs and a close brush with a cul-de-sac, you end up on another boulevard which is really moving along nicely. It's a one-way street and there are fewer stop lights than the streets you've been using. You do so well that you actually arrive at work sooner than usual, despite the slight detour. The next morning you start off for the new boulevard and find that this alternative route gets you to work about ten minutes sooner. You could kick yourself for not having tried it before.

After a little reflection, you feel that you should be a little bit more exploratory in finding routes to and from work, so you try out a few other routes. You don't find anything better but at least now you have alternatives in case your new route gets plugged up some day.

In talking over your experiences with one of your co-workers, you find that if you shift your working day a half-hour forward you can do as well in the morning and hit a low in traffic on the way home. *You end up saving an average of 20 minutes a day*, which adds up to an hour and a half in a week.

Don't Wait for Detour Signs

You are well pleased. *You have proven to yourself that exploring alternatives is good practice*, and you find yourself doing it now on other tasks. You have discovered that it is easy to fall into a comfortable rut and not look for alternatives for routine things.

You know now that there always are alternatives and that some of these will save you time. You know also that circumstances change so that there is always the possibility of finding a better alternative again.

DOING IT THE EASY WAY

There is a lot to be said for getting on with the job. The sooner you start, the sooner you finish—well, almost always. But stop! Pull up on the reins of your eager horse! Instead of dashing off in all directions, figure out how you are going to get there.

You could be OK if it is a routine task and you are not trying to do more in less time. *But habit is a time trap when circumstances have changed.* There may now be an easier way, as there is for the person who finds a faster route to work.

Whenever you are starting something new, it is a good time to look at alternatives, especially when you see a big time commitment ahead of you. You press yourself to think of three or more alternatives. **For an investment of five minutes in creative thought, you may get a big dividend of hours of time saved.**

With the Alternatives Principle, you should be aware that:

1. You need to break out of the time trap of routines.
2. A new task is an opportunity to be creative in finding the easiest way to do it.

SIX ACTIVITIES IN WHICH YOU CAN SHORTEN THE TIME

1. *Reading Your Mail*

One routine activity which cannot be delegated is that of reading your mail. You must make decisions on which letters to answer, which reports to comment on, and which reports are worth reading in detail. Besides that, your third class mail includes information about interesting seminars, and trade news on which you try to keep up to date. Let us suppose that you are stuck with this reading activity but it is beginning to take a lot of precious time. Here are eight alternatives that can save you time.

EIGHT WAYS TO SAVE TIME IN HANDLING YOUR MAIL

1. Secretary open all mail and flatten it out.
2. Have secretary do number 1 and sort into piles of first class and third class mail.
3. Have secretary open, flatten and use her judgment in putting them into three piles of urgent, important and of interest. Allow her the right to discard junk mail.

4. Have a subordinate screen your third class mail and report on things that you could be interested in.

5. Have secretary get your name off lists for external third class mail that you don't want.

6. Have secretary get your name off internal mailings which are for information only.

7. Have a policy to discourage other managers and subordinates from sending you copies of letters that are not of vital concern to you.

8. Encourage people to correspond directly to subordinates, who in turn will inform you of important matters.

With all of these alternatives before you, you will surely find an alternative which will save you time while still achieving an adequate performance level. Obviously, some of these involve the investment of more resources such as that of your secretary and subordinates. Some involve the investment of time on your part in order to get policies changed. The "best" alternative will depend on your particular circumstances.

When I first applied this principle to reading my mail, I managed a complaint investigation team. I saved at least 30 minutes a day.

2. Alternatives for Mining the Periodicals

Most managers and executives have **business periodicals or trade journals to scan in order to keep up to date in their business and to know about trends**. A president I know gets two financial newspapers every week and six trade journals every month. He also subscribes to the Harvard Business Review which comes every second month. He likes to scan the financial papers to know about economic, business, and government trends. From the trade journals he gets as much from the advertisements of competitive merchandise as he does from the how-to articles. To keep abreast of management techniques he usually reads something in the Harvard Business Review. When he is very busy, his reading piles up and he feels very guilty if he doesn't get it done. Sometimes he takes it home and sometimes he stays late to do what he considers a necessary part of his job.

Suppose we apply the Alternatives Principle to the president's problem of mining the periodicals. We will develop a list of alternatives and look for one in which time can be saved without a significant reduction in the performance level. Here is a list that might apply in a typical case:

EIGHT WAYS TO SAVE TIME WITH PERIODICALS
1. Cut down on subscriptions.
2. Read only when there is time to spare.
3. Read while travelling by using public transportation instead of car.
4. Have secretary scan and mark them.
5. Have a subordinate scan the periodicals and mark them.
6. Have subordinates who already scan periodicals mark them.
7. Subscribe to a digest service.
8. Eliminate the reading and do research when some specific information is needed.

Now you have a list of ways to save time without cutting down on the performance level. Some ideas save time by assigning other resources to the activity. Eliminating the scanning of periodicals might save time without loss of performance—if you are just satisfying your curiosity. Besides the additional alternatives with tradeoffs between performance, time, and cost—there are combinations of the above which you can explore. With all these alternatives, you can surely find one which will save you 30 minutes every week. One of my consulting colleagues saved 2 hours a week.

3. Dealing with a Problem Employee

Now consider an intermittent problem. The one selected this time is that of a "problem" employee. Suppose one of your employees has been disturbing another department quite a bit with his comments on their capability. He is nevertheless a valued employee and his work requires him to coordinate projects with other departments. This is a touchy situation and you could easily see it taking a couple of hours of your time. It must be done soon but this is the time of year when you are busy from dawn to dusk with budget preparations and executive meetings. What are the alternatives? Here is a sample of a list you might develop:

ALTERNATIVES TO HANDLE A PROBLEM EMPLOYEE

1. Have personnel department do the corrective interview.
2. Do it in the morning before the panic buttons are pushed.
3. Do it in the late afternoon just before the end of the day.
4. Take employee with you to your golf game and discuss it at the 19th hole.
6. Ask the employee to prepare a self-review and to discuss it with his co-workers before seeing you (high on performance and low on time required of you).
7. Let problem continue for a while and perhaps it will solve itself.

So now you have alternatives and if you combine some of these the list can at least be doubled. Given the circumstances of a particular situation you would find a way to save yourself an hour by using the Alternatives Principle.

4. *Settling a Jurisdictional Dispute*

No organization runs so smoothly that there isn't the occasional jurisdictional dispute which requires your time. It might be an overlap of product planning responsibility between engineering and marketing—or it might be a labour problem between the electricians and the carpenters.

Suppose that in this case a formal grievance has been filed by the union about a higher grade of work being done by persons in a lower classification. Before attending the meeting you might explore the alternatives and consider how they will affect the drain on your time and that of the other members of the organization.

TIME VARYING WAYS TO HANDLE A FORMAL GRIEVANCE ON PAY RATES

- Capitulate and hope for the best (least amount of time lost).
- Don't give in and hope that they back down (probably a moderate amount of time).
- Stall it by one means or another until cooler heads prevail (this might be time consuming).
- Take it to official arbitration and right up to the highest court if necessary. Fight to the bitter end (this will involve a lot of executive time and managerial talent).
- Propose to split the rate difference (you might be lucky and get agreement).
- Put more mechanization into the disputed job so that the classification can be downgraded (this will require some resources and some technical time).

If you proceed with the above, you will not only expand the range of possible solutions to the problem, but if time happens to be precious to you, you can avoid the loss of too much time over a situation where tempers and egos will be deeply involved.

5. *Preparing and Making a Presentation when Time Is Scarce*

For a group activity, I have selected a situation where you are required to make a special presentation to an important meeting. You know from experience that preparation of an important presentation takes a considerable amount of your time. You want to do a good job and keep up your reputation for making clear and entertaining presentations. However, this is the time of the year when your time is at a premium. What are the alternatives?

ALTERNATIVES FOR PREPARING AND MAKING A PRE-SENTATION

1. Have subordinate ghost-write speech and prepare visuals (low performance, low on time).
2. You could write your own speech (high performance, high on time).
3. You could dictate an outline and your ghost-writer could polish it up (use of machine and human resources—reducing the time with only a slight reduction in performance).
4. You can revise the presentation or not depending on the amount of new content.
5. You can use an up-dating of last year's presentation.
6. Subordinate can present the whole thing.
7. Subordinate can present part and you can summarize.

There are more alternatives. Once you get to thinking about the possibilities, the list can be lengthened by combining items. More imaginative schemes can be developed by "free wheeling". This means that **you do not criticize your ideas until you have a complete list**. Since this is a private exercise, there is no reason for you to criticize your own ideas. Free wheeling will enable you to get at other interesting possibilities that lie buried well below the conscious mind. Who knows what ideas might spring forth? This might be the time to have some video film made of the work in progress, and then comment on it. You could arrange to have a portable video tape recorder delivered to the offices of the executives who will attend the meeting. They could preview your presentation. Because of your imagination everyone would knock off early for golf and you would be a hero. As I said, free wheeling is to explore the imagination without criticism until you have it out. That is exactly what I have done. Judgment can be applied after the idea is out.

6. *Handling Ad Hoc Committee Meetings that Rob You of Time*

Suppose you have been told to be part of a special ad hoc committee which is to investigate means of working a shorter week while the same amount of work gets done. Suppose also that you are not the personnel manager. You know that you are redundant because the real work will be done by someone else. Your problem is *how to handle this one with the minimum expenditure of your valuable time*. You are not sure that you can do anything about it, but you have a free-wheeling brainstorm. Using your imagination you write down some ideas without criticizing yourself. They might look as follows:

EIGHT WAYS TO MINIMIZE TIME LOST IN MEETINGS WHICH BARELY CONCERN YOU

1. Forget to go to some of the meetings.
2. Take trade journals along to read during meetings.
3. Insist that the meetings be strictly limited to 30 minutes in a week.

4. Ask the committee chairman to keep you on standby and call you only when needed.

5. Have your secretary go and make notes for you.

6. Stand up to the person who ordered you to be on the committee. Refuse to go.

7. Ask your boss to go instead.

8. Offer to buy the luncheon if they can hold the meetings during the lunch break.

Well, you have a list and you can now apply judgment to the list. It is apparent that in some situations some of these free-wheeling ideas are not going to work. You might be the loser. On the other hand, instead of just submitting to the waste of time, you try to do something about it by using the old noodle to figure out alternative ways that can save you time. A 50% reduction of time is possible with every little effort.

DEVELOP A CONSCIOUSNESS OF ALTERNATIVES

Social pressures tend to make you do the first thing that comes to mind rather than to sit back and ponder the alternatives. Therefore, you must make a conscious attempt to develop this capacity. I have known of this principle for twenty years, but find that I still need to consciously remind myself of it. Moreover, I find that I am applying it in new areas where I previously had not, making me well aware that it's difficult to overcome habitual ways of doing things. My most frequently used self-question is, **"What are the Alternatives?"**.

The Alternatives Principle can become your tool if you practice its application on some of the activities you are currently engaged in. When you constantly surprise yourself at the value you get from developing alternatives, you will eventually become the master of the principle.

GUIDE TO TIME MASTERY

THE ALTERNATIVES PRINCIPLE

There are always alternative ways to shorten the time for a task. They are: by lowering the level of performance; by investing more human or material resources; by creating new procedures.

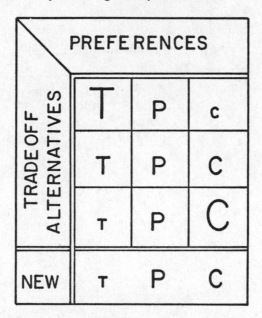

Main Points:
1. There are alternatives which reduce time by using more resources.
2. There are alternatives which reduce time by reducing the performance level.
3. There are sometimes creative method improvements which reduce the time without loss in performance.
4. Alternatives are increased by combining ideas.

Guidelines

1. Identify new activities which have become more or less regular and occupy significant portions of your time. Select a time consuming one and list alternative ways of doing it. Force yourself to list at least five alternatives. (This will be difficult if you have not done it before.) While doing this, consider the possibilities for saving time by reducing the performance or by assigning more resources to the activity.

2. Go into the free-wheeling mode for the activity listed above and extend your list to at least ten. Any idea goes, whether it's workable or not. Reading a list with some screwball ideas in it may trigger a new idea which is both creative and workable. (When you are good at this you will be able to readily fill a page with 30 alternatives for any activity or task. Some people say that the really creative ideas don't begin until after you have 17. This must be tempered with the fact that unless you have been trained in creative techniques you probably will not reach 17 ideas.)

3. Write down an activity in your personal life that takes considerable time which you would like to reduce. Make a list of alternatives as above and try to find one which will reduce the time, is workable, and pleases you.

4. Make a statement of the alternatives principle as you now understand it and do it in your own words. This exercise is to improve your awareness of the alternatives principle.

TIME CHECKLIST TO MASTER THIS PRINCIPLE

Referring to your list of activity and task descriptions as mentioned in chapter 1, ask yourself the following questions for each activity or task:

1. What are the alternatives?
2. Which of these alternatives will save me time without significant loss of performance?
3. Which of these will save me time with a modest drop in performance?
4. Are there any other alternatives which would come about through applying resources to more modern equipment or by upgrading programs for subordinates?

6

How to do Two Things at Once: A Key to Time Management

KEY IDEA:
Gain time by combining activities which by themselves do not fully occupy all of your capabilities—using the Addition Principle.

READING WHILE LISTENING IS RUDE?

Imagine that you are observing the following situation in which a district sales manager looks in at the marketing manager's door and says, "Hank, can we take time to discuss a problem I'm having with the Apex Company?"

"Sure, John, c'mon in and sit down. . . . Now tell me about the problem."

While John is talking and bringing Hank up to date, the marketing manager is going through a pile of mail on his desk. He is reading letters, putting notes on them and looking at reports. Some work he sets aside and other work he completes. John continues to talk as if Hank is completely absorbed in what he is telling him. John doesn't seem annoyed at the actions of the marketing manager. The moment John finishes the background information on the problem,

111

Hank asks an incisive question which indicates that he clearly understood. Then Hank tells him about a similar problem they have with another customer. While he is doing this, John picks up a trade magazine and scans its contents. Hank is not annoyed and continues on.

What we see is apparently rude behavior on the part of two persons toward one another. Neither gives the other full attention. But let's look a little further. Is full attention needed to discuss a customer that both know something about? Is the information really that new and breathtaking that the other person should sit at the edge of his seat with anticipation? Not likely. We notice also in this situation that if one person reads while listening, then the other person is able to do the same.

What is really going on is that *these people are making use of the difference between speaking rate and comprehension rate.* A fast reader can comprehend 600 words per minute, but a fast talker can't do better than 200 words per minute. An average talker is only putting out about 100 words per minute. An intelligent manager can comprehend at least three times that in complex reading, and six to ten times that in material he is familiar with. Thus the listener has only about one-third of his capacity utilized. The other two-thirds of his mind can be put into reading magazines or mail of low consequence—a gain of 40 minutes in every hour of listening! Neither task requires his undivided attention—so both can be done at the same time.

We see the kind of time awareness that can be developed between managers and subordinates. When the subordinate knows for certain that the manager can listen and do other work at the same time, then that person is not offended by it. The subordinate in this case knows for sure that if he has something new that requires the undivided attention of the marketing manager, he will get it. That is why John does not feel that Hank is being rude. Thus, when people are working together and are concerned about the performance level of the team as a whole, they can accommodate situations such as the above.

There are many cases where people can do two tasks at the same time and employ the Addition Principle which is elaborated below.

WHAT YOU WILL GAIN FROM THIS CHAPTER

The Addition Principle means to do two or more tasks in the time required for one. A very common use of this principle is by the person who takes some reports to study while travelling.

There are many activities that do not fully occupy your capacities. It costs nothing more to use all of your capacities than it does to use part of them. At one extreme, a routine task done at the subconscious habitual level can be boring. Combining two boring tasks may bring the work up to the interesting level. Working life and personal life are full of examples where people are doing two or more things at once but are not conscious of the Addition Principle. When you understand this principle, then you can apply it to your work situation and save time by combining tasks that can be done together.

BENEFITS OF USING THE ADDITION PRINCIPLE

1. You will be able to combine some tasks and accomplish more within a fixed amount of time.
2. You will make use of otherwise wasted time.
3. Boring activities can become interesting when using the Addition Principle.
4. You will be able to employ more of your human capacities instead of having them under used part of the time.
5. You will enjoy the challenge of combining tasks and bringing yourself to new levels of accomplishment.

This chapter, like the one on the Alternatives Principle, deals with the efficient use of time. Immediately following are a few of the finer points of the Addition Principle. Why it works is explained. Then you are shown how to apply it and enjoy your travelling to and from work. Another situation shows how if you are cooling your heels for an appointment you can grab this gift of free time and use it.

This chapter contains five time-saving techniques for applying the Addition Principle to your work by using a portable tape recorder; by reading while listening; by taking advantage of the undisturbed time of a long air trip or an evening in your hotel room; by making meeting times more productive.

Finally, you are shown how to make this principle your life long servant by applying it to your list of activities and tasks.

THE ADDITION PRINCIPLE

If you combine tasks and get full results in less time than it would take to do the tasks separately, then you have saved time under the Addition Principle.

A simple example is to combine lunch and exercise times. One hour is usually allowed for lunch, and doctors advise exercise for one half hour in a day. Total 1½ hours. Use the stairs instead of the elevator and take a vigorous talk to a nearby restaurant. Both activities can be completed in one hour. Time saved—one half hour.

There follow a few extensions of the Addition Principle which can help you better understand and apply it to your use of time.

Case 1: You are waiting for the doctor and have nothing to do. The time, T_1, exists but nothing is being accomplished, so the performance P_1 equals zero. If during this time you study reports or practice recalling customers' names, you get something for your time, say performance P_2. Note that the Addition Principle only applies when something is accomplished towards your purposes. If, while waiting to see the doctor, you pick up any old magazine just to fill in the time, you may have done two things at once but nothing was accomplished towards your purposes.

Case 2: Suppose you are to do a task which will achieve performance level P_1, and can be done in time T_1. If you now use T_1 to accomplish something else with performance level P_2, then you will have accomplished $P_1 + P_2$. An example of Case 2 would be travelling and studying. Travel is an accomplishment because if you are required to get from A to B you cannot possibly do this in zero time. Studying presumably also contributes to your purposes. Note that we need to look again at purposes and not at the activity. When both activities contribute simultaneously towards your purposes, then you are applying the Addition Principle.

Of course, not all activities can be combined. When one fully occupies your capabilities there is no capacity left for another. Even when two activities together do not fully occupy your capabilities, it may take some practice to develop the capacity to do both at the same time without some loss in quality.

Case 3: Suppose the time, T_1, used for doing a task with performance level P_1, is also used for accomplishing P_2, P_3, P_4 and so on. In other words, more than two tasks are combined in the time T_1; or at least, the final time is less than the sum of individual times would have been. This use of the Addition Principle is difficult to come by but occasionally happens. For example, one may walk to work in the same time it would take to drive and park, thereby getting some necessary exercise as well as getting from A to B. On such a routine route it is possible for your subconscious to direct your feet. Your mind can be actively employed in solving problems or exercising the memory. Thus, three things may be accomplished in the time of one.

Case 4: Doing one task may aid the doing of another task in such a way that both are done together in less time than it takes to do either. This is the big discovery you make when applying the Addition Principle.

So much for examples of the Addition Principle. It is

now possible to make a general statement about it as follows:

THE ADDITION PRINCIPLE

More than one task can be done during the same time period when the capacity required for each task is less than all of your natural plus machine-augmented capacities.

The sub-principles are as follows:
1. The tasks should have utility with respect to your purposes.
2. The principle can be extended to the case where the new time taken is more than the time for one task but still less than the sum of the times for all tasks done separately.
3. Some tasks can be done better when combined than when done separately.

P_1	P_2	$P_1 + P_2$
T_1	T_2	T_1
□	○	◻○
✌	👂	👂 👁 👁 👂

SAVE TIME THROUGH THESE EVERYDAY USES OF THE ADDITION PRINCIPLE

Enjoy Your Travelling to and from Work

Luck is how you see it. Lucky is the person who is not required to travel to work or who can get there in a few minutes. Lucky also is the person who spends two hours in every working day just travelling to and from the job. This person has a marvelous opportunity to usefully employ the travelling time. The unlucky person is the one who sees the travel as a burden to be borne in a working life, the only relief in sight being retirement.

How much time do you spend in travelling? A total of one hour a day is certainly not unusual. There are roughly 240 working days in a year, so that comes out to 240 hours—six continuous weeks at 40 hours a week! That's a lot of time. If only part of this time is available for exercising the mind and body, then it's worth looking at. The Addition Principle is one to apply here. **Put it to full use and you will gain up to six weeks in a year**.

First of all, when you arrive at your destination, you have accomplished a task that can never be done in zero time. However, the significant thing about routine travelling is that it becomes habitual. Your mind and body are not absorbed to capacity. If you drive to work over a regular route, your turns and stops are semi-automatic. In fact, they are so automatic that it's hard to break the habit and change the route. If you travel by public transport you will get so that you act like a robot. Whether you sleep, read, or waste the time in small talk, you will automatically know when it is time to get off.

I have noticed that some people sleep on the bus or train. This can be like putting sleep in the bank at the end of the day, but it is not much use in the morning when you have just awakened. Extra sleep may pass the time, but unless you need it, it accomplishes nothing towards your purposes. On the other hand, some people read the morning newspaper on the way into work and the evening newspaper on the way back. Boredom is reduced. Newspapers are full of interesting stories about three-headed calves, or violence.

They are meant to get your attention. (Occasionally I go through an orgy of newspaper reading myself. Then a week later I try to recall some of the things that I have read—I find it is next to nothing.) As long as one is just going to read, why not read something that contributes to one's purposes?

When Your Mind, Eyes and Hands are Free

There are two situations to consider. The first situation is when you are being transported and your mind, eyes and hands are completely free for a good part of the time. You can do some serious reading of things like magazines that help you in your work, because you can make notes. You can study something like a language or mathematics, which you can do in silence and not disturb other persons. You can also take along your pleasure reading because there will be times when you are not in the mood for serious reading. It's best to **have a variety of things with you** because the circumstances of travel are not always that regular.

It is good to have something that can be done while standing as well as sitting. For standing work I find that **little 3 × 5 cards with notes are very handy as cue cards**. I can glance at these while waiting for transport or while standing in a crowded subway. These are usually things that I like to memorize. The beautiful thing that I have found about having something serious to do while travelling is that the time seems so much shorter. Circumstances and other passengers do not annoy me. My body is there but my mind is somewhere else. On the other hand, if I want to, I can admire the scenery out the window or about me in the vehicle. This is so infrequent that when I do look at the scenery it appears like an original experience.

When You Are Driving

The second situation of travelling is where you are the driver. Then your hands, eyes, and mind can be well occupied. At other times you are driving along a boulevard or freeway and your subconscious mind takes over. You can be listening to the radio and beating one hand to the music. As long as your eyes are on the road you are probably a better driver than the one who is getting drowsy from boredom. Some of the things I have found that one can do while driving the car in routine fashion (not in busy traffic—ever!) follow.

SIXTEEN THINGS YOU CAN DO WHILE ENGAGED IN VERY ROUTINE DRIVING

1. Learning songs from tapes.
2. Learning a language from tapes.
3. Tapes about selling and management.
4. Tapes about time management.
5. Counting to 100 in five languages.
6. Dictating taped correspondence.
7. Dictating letters or articles.
8. Studying other cars when considering a new one.
9. Planning for the day ahead.
10. Reviewing the workday gone by.
11. Mulling over problems (not worrying).
12. Eating a snack.
13. Having fresh coffee brewed in the car (I prefer to stop for a moment while pouring).
14. Isometric exercises (you can push on the dash, pull in opposite directions on the steering wheel, push against the seat, flex stomach muscles).
15. Arm exercise with a small dumbbell.
16. Finger strengthening exercises.

What you can do during routine travelling is up to your imagination. A small amount of additional activity can actually increase your alertness. You need to be able to drop what you are doing instantly if the traffic situation changes—something I used to be reluctant to do, but learned to do with practice.

2. Grab that Gift of Time While Waiting for your Appointment

In the doctor's waiting room even the high nobles are reduced to lowly serfs. The prince of medicine keeps you in his audience hall until your turn has come. If your appointment is for 3 p.m. you will consider yourelf lucky if you see the doctor by 3:30. If instead you come at 3:30, you may not see him until 4:30. If you are in any kind of a hurry, don't expect the doctor to pay any attention to your need. Busy executives and idle retirees wait in the same lineup. As you move up in priority you may be lucky enough to move into an examining room and strip off all of your identity as a person. This may help the doctor with managing his time, and it may help him be objective with each patient—but it is seldom an efficient use of time for the kind of person who reads this book.

To reduce your frustration at waiting for your appointment, some nice doctors have provided reading material for you—such as excellently bound copies of the Windsdowne Ladies' Checkers Society Annual Reports, copies of Luxury Travel Abroad, and if you're lucky—even a few comic books. If, on the other hand, you are waiting for the dentist, then reading something may reduce your apprehension. The dentist will provide books on oral hygiene with great big gaping mouths and sorry looking teeth. These are supposed to make you feel so happy about taking care of your teeth that you can hardly wait for the drilling to start.

Take Your Reading Material With You

Anyway, the long and short of it is that *there are many situations where you simply must wait*: like going to the barber; waiting while your spouse shops; and waiting for service in a busy restaurant. When you add this all up, the average person has at least an hour a week of waiting time which adds up to a good healthy fifty hours in a year. Fifty hours in a year is like a whole working week and will go a long way toward your self development. Is there something you would like to learn? Are you reading up on your hobby? Would you like to brush up on another language? Would you like to answer some overdue letters? The procedure is simple. **You select what you want to achieve during your annual waiting time and put it in a plastic briefcase.** Take it with you when you know you are going to be waiting.

Waiting time, as a rule, puts us in a position where we

accomplish nothing towards our purposes. We fidget around, get apprehensive or even angry. This is not good. Instead of that, decide what is going to be your worthwhile activity for your waiting time and plan to have something with you. When you do this, instead of being angry you may even welcome the long lineup for a haircut because of what you can accomplish during that quiet uninterrupted time.

3. Some Things That are Better When Done Together

Dancing is a neat way to combine social activity, exercise and courtship, thereby adding together three things which could have been done separately, but are better done when combined. Like jam and peanut butter on a sandwich, some things go together better than separately.

In the application of the Addition Principle to group activities, some useful combinations happen by chance. For example, a friend of mine promised his wife one riské joke per day. He tapped the joke-of-the-day grapevine at the cafeteria. He regularly exchanged a story with cafeteria personnel while lining up for coffee and donuts—a neat combination of friendship, information gathering, and snacking.

With the Addition Principle you should be aware that:
1. Activities that do not fully occupy your capacity can be combined and done at the same time.
2. Waiting time and travel time are good places to add on other accomplishments.
3. Doing two things at once is frequently better for both than doing one thing at a time.

FIVE TIME SAVING TECHNIQUES

1. What a Portable Tape Recorder Can Do for You

Most managers and executives spend a substantial portion of their day in travel. They tend to live in suburbs, travel alone in a car, and be obliged to take a number of business trips. It's a great pleasure for an executive to drive home in his car and have a little bubble of space to himself with no intrusions by telephones or other executives. An even better situation is having a chauffeur driven limousine with a stereo and bar. However, given that the ideal is still to be achieved by most, what can be done by an executive who spends considerable time travelling in a car?

There is one piece of machinery which, when added to a car plus executive, equals fun and effectiveness. That is a portable tape recorder. The small pocket-sized dictating machines are reasonably priced and available. They fit in your hand. They can be carried in your pocket, purse, or briefcase and can be with you at all times.

For the person who likes deluxe options with a car, there are cassette installations which can be dash mounted. The microphone can be held in a dash receptacle and have a flexible cord. It can also be hung from the ceiling or hung around the neck like telephone answering headsets.

For the up and coming manager who forks out his own money, there are excellent low cost cassette recorders with piano-type keys. They can be operated on the car seat.

The microphone used in a car should be a separate unit unless it is part of a hand-size recorder. You need one that can come close to the mouth because of car noises and traffic noises. You can tether it to your clothing or to the sun visor so that you can drop it at a moment's notice and grab the steering wheel without damaging the microphone. Another technicality is that you need to have a means of switching it on and off.

What can the portable tape recorder do for the executive or manager? Plenty! Here are 13 of those things.

13 WAYS TO ACCOMPLISH MORE WITH THE USE OF A PORTABLE TAPE RECORDER

1. Make notes on meetings just attended.
2. Follow up letters.
3. Drafts of reports.

4. Instant capturing of ideas. Have your secretary type them on 3 × 5 cards.

5. Memos to secretary.

6. Dictate complaints about road conditions.

7. Self-instruction by cassettes on management, time mastery, selling, delegation, etc.

8. Mind-stretching point of view talks recorded by well-known persons.

9. Learning another language.

10. Correspondence to and from friends.

11. Meetings with yourself to verbalize problem situations.

12. Listening to music of your own choice.

13. Review your speeches.

Please note that many of the above things can also be done while travelling by air or subway, or while waiting at the airport. You need not be too shy about dictating in an aircraft as it is becoming fairly commonplace. (I like it best though when the seats beside me are vacant.)

Don R., a manager I know, used his pocket recorder to record his ideas about a problem and had them transcribed. When a meeting was held to discuss it he surprised himself and his fellow managers by the number of useful ideas that he presented.

2. How to Capitalize on the Reading and Listening Speed Differential

There are ways you can capitalize on the fact that people can read at least three times as fast as they can speak. This fact means that you can comprehend something at three times the rate at which a person can speak. Even a person who speaks fast will have difficulty maintaining 200 words per minute and this rate is very slow for reading.

Let's take a look at a few possibilities. For example, if

you are away from your office for an extended period of time, **ask your secretary to type up details of telephone messages that are left for you**. This will take a little bit more of her time but she is usually not busy when you are away. When you come back you can very rapidly scan the messages. You call on your secretary for more details only when necessary.

You can frequently **scan trade journals or routine letters and reports while you are listening to a telephone conversation**. You keep a pile of reading or work material which requires low attention. It is within reach of your telephone. With a little practice you can develop your capacity to listen and read at the same time without any loss to either activity. Do not attempt to combine high attention reading with telephone conversations until you have developed a high degree of skill. Practice with routine reading material during the talk by a long-winded caller. Then you will find out what you are able to do with the capacities you have.

Suppose you listen for two hours in a business day, and that one hour of this is familiar to you. If you do routine reading during this time, you can use the two-thirds of your comprehending ability that would otherwise be wasted. That comes to 40 minutes of gained time in a day!

3. Take Advantage of that Undisturbed Time that you get on a Long Air Trip

In this jet age of rapid air travel, the executive saves time when he travels by air but he also usually goes to more places. Consequently, many persons are not looking forward to their next long air trip. Apart from changing meal and sleep schedules, there is the matter of three to ten hours in one seat in the kind of confinement that an executive does not experience on the regular job. One can listen to music; watch the movies; dilly-dally over the main meal; read airline magazines; or just get drunk. There are various solutions to problems of air-travel boredom. Increasingly though, executives who travel by air are taking work with them—either in their briefcase or in their minds. The holiday makers can relieve their boredom in the ways provided by the airliine, but the persons who are focusing on accomplishment cannot afford to let these precious hours go to waste.

I met one person on a flight who told me that he **deliberately set aside work which would take him two to three hours** so that he could do it during an airline trip. Another person, a marketing manager, had his calculator with him for planning his pricing strategy. He looked forward to having time to plan.

As for myself, I am generally looking forward to a long air trip because of the hours of uninterrupted time which will be mine to use. On the morning trips **I generally write reports, proposals or articles**. It was during one five-hour trip that I developed the scientific reasoning for the management of time. I found the accomplishment exhilarating.

Air travel can also be **a way of putting sleep in the bank if properly planned**. When I am travelling from east to west I must stay up later than usual and I use the airplane to log up one or two hours of sleep. What I do may not always please the airlines, but I come prepared. I use various inflatable beach balls and pillows to make myself comfortable in whatever space I have available. If I can find three seats together near the rear of the aircraft, I lie down. On jumbo-jets I can occasionally find a place to stretch out my full six feet. I find that two hours napping in the aircraft is equivalent at least to one hour of sleep in a hotel. It also gives me a chance to **start adjusting for jet lag**—that change in living routine that is required by a different time zone.

4. What to do when Stuck in Your Hotel Room

When out of town on a business trip the evenings are not always full of entertainment. Frequently a manager will find several full evenings available all to himself. There are many ways of using this found time. You can frequent the bar and I'm not going to knock it if that's your bag. In some hotels you can watch movies in your room, for a fee, of course. You can also head off for the nightclubs.

What the movies show the executive doing when he is out of town and what he is actually doing are quite different. The executive who is successful is usually a well-balanced person who gets adequate recreation with family and friends on the weekends. When in a hotel he is not going to waste those valuable uninterrupted evening hours.

Long-range planning is the most neglected part of an executive's job and here is a chance to put things right. **You plan to plan—and have those things available with you that will make it easy to do.** Planning requires that you write and that's why you plan to do it in a hotel room, whereas casual reading can be done while you are travelling in a vehicle.

The evenings are long, and two hours of planning tends to make one a bit foggy. What else to do? Well, for one thing, many hotels are equipped with swimming pools and saunas. While you are away from home you are not getting the regular exercise that is probably part of your program. Now is the chance to have a little workout in the pool or a vigorous walk around town. **You put some exercise in the bank,** so to speak, so that you will have more free time on the weekend when you are at home. Not a bad idea too, because while away from home you are often wining and dining quite heavily and you have those extra calories to burn off. If, by chance, you are mulling over your planning programs while taking your vigorous walks and also waiting for the next business day, then you are pretty close to doing three things at once.

5. How to get the Most out of Meetings

Meetings are for managers like bread is for peasants. They are necessary but also commonplace. How can you make meetings have additional utility with respect to your purposes? Let me suggest a few.

Take the case where you must **contact a fellow manager** about something that will take only two or three minutes to discuss. He is busy when you call and you leave a message with his secretary. When he calls back you are away at a meeting and so now it's your turn to call him. After two days you wish you had written a letter—but it is a touchy matter and you must do it face-to-face. You deliberately drop by his office just after lunch and find that he won't be back that afternoon. Cripes! This little matter is getting important because it involves a personality clash between one of his people and one of yours. How to handle it? You may have to call him up at his home, a thing that both of you dislike. Then you remember that there is a departmental meeting every Thursday afternoon. You decide to arrive a couple of minutes early to see your colleague. You send a note to his secretary to ask him to do the same thing. **You sit next to each other and during the preliminaries you are able to discuss and settle this little problem. You do in three minutes what would have taken 15.** Now you have a modus operandi that you can use with your colleague simply by planning ahead. Probably he will use these regular meetings to take matters up with you as well.

There is another use of meetings which you can make work for you. Many times you are called upon to make a presentation and this is one of the skills that you wish to develop. Nobody can be so good at it that they can't improve a little. How to get improvement? You can join Toastmasters, or you can practice in front of a mirror—but nothing is better than a little feedback in a real situation. You make arrangements with your colleague to give you little signals as to whether you should talk louder, faster, funnier, etc. He slips you a little note to say that your hands are covering up your visual displays. **A little feedback from your colleague will make each presentation better.** You will be developing better style as you progress. Naturally, you will want to do the same for your colleague, which is a **good way to build**

teamwork. Presenting; improving; team-building;—three things at once! By doing this I saved one evening a week which formerly went to public speaking practice with the Toastmasters' Club.

TO SAVE MORE TIME—FOLLOW THROUGH WITH THE ADDITION PRINCIPLE

You can see from the examples and techniques above that there are many practical ways for you to use this principle. However, the important thing is to learn the principle itself rather than the specific techniques. **When you know the principle, then you can apply it in many other situations** which couldn't possibly all be mentioned in this book. When you have developed time awareness you will want to relate priorities to purposes and to budget your time. When you are planning what you are actually going to do, that is the time to start combining things. Remember that the Addition Principle applies mainly to those tasks which don't use all of your capacities.

It is often said that you cannot do two things at once. This is not true, because you can obviously use different sensory inputs at the same time when they are not fully occupied. Different sensory inputs frequently go to unconnected parts of the mind, and can thus be operated more or less independently. Moreover, the subconscious mind takes over control of habitual behavior such as walking and routine driving. People who don't understand the psychological makeup of man often say, "Do one thing at a time and do it until it is completed". This sort of advice is good for the person who is simple-minded and unorganized. But you, the sophisticated manager or executive, wish to make multiple uses of your senses.

You, as an achiever, should not be satisfied until you have experienced the euphoria of discovering that you can do three things at once!

THE ADDITION PRINCIPLE

More than one task can be done during the same time period when the capacity required for each task is less than all of your natural plus machine-augmented capacities.

The sub-principles are as follows:
1. All combined tasks should have utility with respect to your purposes.
2. The principle can be extended to the case where the new time taken is more than the time for one task but still less than the sum of the times for all tasks done separately.
3. Some tasks can be done better when combined than when done separately.

P_1	P_2	$P_1 + P_2$
T_1	T_2	T_1
□	○	◉

Main points:
1. Routine things which can be relegated to habitual behavior can be augmented with conscious behavior of a different type.
2. Many activities use less than your full capacity to learn or produce. You combine low capacity activities.

3. Some activities require your undivided attention and should not be combined with others.

4. Effectiveness in combining activities increases with practice.

5. If you can do two things at once, why not three?

TIME CHECKLIST TO MASTER THIS PRINCIPLE

1. Refer to a copy of the checklist which you started in chapter 1 and elaborated with additional tasks which apply uniquely to your job. For each of these, mark them as low (L) capacity requirements and high (H) on capacity requirements.

2. Look at the ones which are low on capacity requirements. Do some of them use different sensory inputs? If so, can they be combined?

3. Among the ones that use low amounts of total capacity, are there some that can be relegated to habitual behavior and combined with a conscious activity?

4. Consider the differential between reading and listening speeds. Are there subordinates who would work with you on learning how to read and listen together in some situations? If so, try it.

7 | A Breakthrough In Time Management: The Multiplication Principle

KEY IDEA:
Make a single effort count for many uses—
using the Multiplication Principle.

MAKE ONE FOR ME TOO

The office manager of a Toronto firm had an idea for improving the efficiency of handling sales records. He looked through the equipment catalogues but didn't find anything that was really suitable, so he hired a carpenter-mechanic to work on his idea. After a number of trials he finally came up with a piece of equipment that did a splendid job. It saved time and it prevented the documents from getting damaged in handling.

A short time later one of the western branch office managers was being shown around on a tour. With pride the office manager showed him the new equipment that he had had specifically built. It really worked well and he was justifiably proud of it. The branch manager agreed, but lamented the fact that he had not known the Toronto office manager was developing this equipment. He had also recognized the need for it, and spent weeks fiddling around until he finally got it to handle his sales records. It was really not a great deal different. Had he known, the Toronto man could have made two of them at the same time. That would have saved a lot of time. Here was a case where one effort could have counted twice and saved time. If more branch offices needed them, the time saving could have been multiplied.

SAVE TIME WITH THE BREAKTHROUGH IN TIME MANAGEMENT

In the case above, you see just one possible use of the Multiplication Principle. That is, one piece of work can be put to more than one use—*a real breakthrough* in efficient time management. Sometimes it requires a slight modification of the format or procedure but the principle is just the same. **You save time again and again** when the results of one piece of work can be put to other uses.

BENEFITS OF USING THE MULTIPLICATION PRINCIPLE ARE:

1. You save time in the future if you can organize a task so that part of the results can be used for another task.
2. Because the time saved can be multiplied many times, the time saved in total can be very large in proportion to the original effort required.
3. Real "breakthroughs" in time management can come about by the creative use of this principle.

In this chapter are the details of the fantastic Multiplication Principle. Why the time saving is multiplied is explained first. Then I tell you how I use the principle in writing this very book—ten uses for one major effort and more to come! We also see how Bernie R. applied the principle to selling.

You will find eight techniques for efficient use of your time in work application, such as: form letters; action copies of letters; bulk buying; modular reports; multiplying the benefits of a consultation; multiple uses for your trip reports; extra benefits from meetings; and multiplying the effect of a reprimand.

You can multiply your uses of the Multiplication Principle when you understand the principle itself, and you can use it again and again in your work and personal life.

THE MULTIPLICATION PRINCIPLE

Suppose there are two tasks to be done. The first task, when completed, will have performance level P_1; cost of materials and resources C_1; and be completed in time T_1. The second task could be defined by P_2, C_2 and T_2. If both tasks are done at separate times then the results achieved are $P_1 + P_2$; the costs have been $C_1 + C_2$; and the elapsed time would be $T_1 + T_2$. If we were able to use the Addition Principle outlined in the previous chapter, then P_1 and P_2 represent two tasks that can be done together, and therefore the total time taken would be only T_1.

The Multiplication Principle is different. Suppose that the tasks, n, are essentially the same, so that in fact the results of the first task, P_1, could be substituted for the performance level of the other tasks. Thus, the overall result would be equal to $n \times P_1$, cost $n \times C_1$, but take only time T_1, once. This is the Multiplication Principle—where uses of results of a particular task may be multiplied many times.

Common everyday uses of this principle are the extra carbon copies you get from typing a letter; and the piece of bent metal that doubles as a bottle opener and can opener. Mass-produced plastic toys are another use of the Multiplication Principle, because one hand-crafted toy can be mass-molded for use by many children.

Actually, as you may have sensed, the Multiplication Principle is not so pure as a formula would lead one to believe. The extra carbon copies in a typewriter are not quite as good as the first. You can't take any old piece of work and multiply its uses. It is usually necessary to invest a little time in the modeling of the form of the first task. In other words, P_1 is so adjusted so that it resembles P_2. In order to get P_1 completed it may take a bit more time and have a bit more cost. However, in the long run, the time taken for completing the first task is much less than for completing both tasks separately. The big payoff comes when we have multiple uses for the results of one piece of work. Then the saving in time is multiplied over and over again and the gains can be enormous. This is the real power in the Multiplication Principle.

We can now make a statement about the principle.

THE MULTIPLICATION PRINCIPLE

A task can sometimes be done in such a way that it contributes substantially to other tasks, thereby saving most of the time required for the other tasks. When the results of the first task have multiple uses, the time saved in the future is multiplied.

FIRST USE	SECOND USE	THIRD USE
Ⓣ	◯	◯
[T]	▢	▢
Ⓣ	▣	◎

HOW I USED THE MULTIPLICATION PRINCIPLE IN WRITING THIS BOOK

What Other Uses Can I Have for this Piece of Work?

This is the question I have constantly asked myself since starting to write about time management. I am getting a lot of mileage from the Multiplication Principle I have developed. Let me list a few.

1. A full length book "The Mastery and Management of Time" for managers, executives and professionals.
2. 30 articles for trade magazines and business newspapers.
3. A regular column for a business trade magazine.
4. After dinner speeches on time mastery.
5. A seminar-workship for presentation to the public and to organizations.
6. A workbook to be sold to licensed trainers who put on the seminar-workshop.
7. A mail-order course on time management.
8. Tape recordings on time management.
9. A film for instruction on time management.
10. Collaborative books on time for vastly different occupations.
11, 12, etc. Other ideas that I am not ready to disclose yet.

At first I started out with two uses—a book and articles. But I keep applying the Multiplication Principle and the end is not in sight yet. What made this possible? Careful planning before writing. Each chapter is more or less independent and can be used for stand-alone articles because it is in modular form.

You, the reader, are the prime beneficiary of the use of the Multiplication Principle in this book. **Because you learn principles instead of reading through the specific tips, you can apply each principle to your activities again and again and again.** You multiply the benefits you get.

Oh yes. I almost forgot to tell you. The other use I am getting for my work is that *I am applying the principles myself—again and again to other activities.* They really work! And since writing this chapter, I have discovered a whole new dimension for multiplying my output. I now have a list of 75 useful products which will use part or all of my original writing!

HOW BERNIE R. MULTIPLIED HIS SELLING EFFORTS

A salesman for office filing systems must do a lot of prospecting to get a customer. Bernie R. would use the telephone directory, and systematically call up companies, trying to get an appointment with the office manager. This was slow going, yielding less than one appointment for a day of effort. From the appointments, only about 1 in 10 resulted in a sale, so nine days of appointment getting was going to waste.

Of ten office managers, at least five were "sold" on his filing system, even if only one was able to buy. So Bernie wondered how he could put this effort to other uses. He started asking for referrals from those who "bought the idea." This worked. Instead of a wasted day in prospecting and another wasted day explaining the merits of his system, he at least got some referrals for his effort. So out of ten selling visits, he averaged one sale plus ten referrals, which usually resulted in another sale. He doubled his sales and saved half of his prospecting time.

SEVEN TIME SAVING WAYS TO USE THE MULTIPLICATION PRINCIPLE

1. Save Time on Correspondence by Keeping a File of Modular Letters

A lot of the work of correspondence is in composing a very careful reply. You may draft up something and revise it a couple of times. This is part of your creative output and can be put in the bank for future uses.

What you need to do is to take the idea of the form letter and extend it into unique and different letters. This is done by composing a letter in **modular paragraphs** that do not include the name of the receiver. The paragraphs discuss the subject matter. For example, instead of saying . . . "Mrs. Jones, we have examined your returned merchandise on order number 17382, and found that the seams were much worse than they should have been" . . . you put the order number in a separate paragraph and say, "We have examined the merchandise returned in your order menditoned above and have found that it is defective as claimed". You may want to work over the general purpose statement so that it doesn't get you into hot water when you use it again.

Later, you simply retrieve a copy of the letter which you have set aside in **a file entitled "Modular Form Letters"**. You dictate the heading and tell your secretary to include paragraph 2 of modular letter 16.

You can extend this principle into proposals or quotations that go out. You write the specifics of the recipient on a covering letter and attach your proposal as an appendix. A proposal can generally be worded so that it is not specific to any one client and deals only with your subject matter. Then you can use the same Proposal with other letters without recomposing—or by changing just a few words.

2. Initiate Action by Several Persons with One Letter

A way to make use of the Multiplication Principle with correspondence is to mention the action required of several persons and send the letter only to the principal person. Here is an example that saves the time of writing two more letters:

P.S. By copy of this letter I am asking that May S. telephone your office and get details of the warranty claim.

I am also requesting that John B. of the Service department grant your claim for extended warranty.

c.c. May S.
John B.

3. Multiply Your Decision on What to Buy. Save on Future Time.

It sometimes happens that the *bulk-buying practices* employed by purchasing departments in large concerns are not applied to the use of office supplies which executives and managers control. Even when the whole stationery budget is delegated to secretaries, there is a tendency to run short of pencils, paper clips, carbon papers, etc. The budget is well under control but key people are wasting time looking for a pencil. Pencils are cheap and salaries are high. Not only should there be adequate office supplies but people should be encouraged to *save time by taking a bulk supply back to their desk.*

Some special purchases are small in the amount of money spent in relation to the time involved, as for example, *choosing a reference book.* So, once the time has been spent making a decision on one of these purchases, it can be multiplied and extended to future purchases of the same thing by going to a bulk-buy for other users. This saves time.

It is possible for you to *extend the bulk-buy principle to your personal purchases.* For example, if you are the person who prefers to buy your own clothing rather than delegate this to a spouse, then you can do a bulk-buy and save time at it. For example, if you see a shirt that you like, why not get three? You'll eventually use three shirts anyway and possibly make two additional trips to find ones which you like just as well as the one which you have just chosen. Besides, if you have three of a kind, one necktie will serve all three, so you have simplified your wardrobe and saved time as well. Extend this to anything you buy, particularly those things that do not require a large capital outlay, but do require a time outlay. *If you are eventually going to spend the money anyway, time is the only thing that you can save.* An exception would be where a large sum of money is required and the interest on the money is important too. For example, in a lifetime you will buy twenty or more cars, but I don't suggest you go out and buy twenty cars at once. That would be carrying the Multiplication Principle too far.

Apply the multiplication in those purchases where there will be a good saving of time in proportion to the money outlay.

4. Modular Reports Save Time in the Long Run

Managers and executives are frequently required to rack their brains and burn the midnight oil to get out special reports. Such occasions require a lot of you and it is only good sense that you should get multiple uses for your effort—so use the modular format.

It is common practice to include an executive summary of the highlights as one module of a report. This gives more uses to the report because *the executive summary may be given a wider circulation* or passed upstairs by the executive who gets the report. Some reports could be given even wider circulation for information purposes, and be helpful to your organization, if there is no confidential material in them. It is frequently possible to *put the confidential material in modules which can be removed* without destroying the sense of the main report.

There are other uses which you can get out of a report. Does it contain material which would be useful as advertising copy? Could a general information bulletin come out of it? Is there a module which could be used for a public relations announcement?

Most reports have **material that can be used again in other reports. Plan in advance for future use**. If there must be a little glue between the modules, use interconnecting paragraphs at the beginning of each, and delete them in future uses.

I have found that the graphics portion of a report usually has multiple uses. I must spend considerable time composing a chart or graph which really communicates. I also employ the valuable time of my secretary and a draftsman to transform my freehand sketch into something reproducible. After my first freehand sketch I think to myself, "What other uses can I put this work to?" Frequently all I need to do is change some of the captions and words and it

is useful for an article or another report. *Whenever any
drafting is done I make two copies of the basic sketch which
can be used again.* One copy is developed for present use,
and the other filed for future use. The same principle
applies to the preparation of visuals. Sometimes a figure for
a report finds multiple uses in other reports, papers, articles,
and in visuals. You can save hours of time on future reports.

*5. Get Top Value for the Time and Money Spent on a Tele-
phone Consultation—Record it and Use it Again*

It is not unusual for a manager or executive to telephone an expert in a far away place and hold a lengthy consultation about a problem. If you do this, the *information is
very valuable because it is coming from an expert and it is
also employing your time. Because it is new to you, your
memory will be less than perfect. Much of what is said you
will want to recall and ponder, and much of it can be useful
to other members of your organization.* To increase its use,
record it. Of course, you record with the other person's consent, just as they allow themselves to be recorded by telephone answering machines. After you have obtained the
consent of the other party, turn on your tape recorder and
say something like "I have just turned the tape recorder on
in order to record our conversation, which is what you agreed to. Right?" The other party assents. They may be a little
cautious in what they say because of being recorded, but
experts shouldn't be giving bad information by the telephone anyway. As far as confidential information goes, few
people will give this by telephone anyway because they can
never be sure whether or not they are being recorded.

Some years ago, in a technical position, I was required
to consult with technical experts about urgent problems by
long distance telephone. I recorded the conversations and
had my secretary type them up. Then I would scan them
through and mark those things that were important to me. I
would use one copy for follow-up and one for the file. Frequently other people were involved in the problem and
needed some of the information, so I would take other

copies and mark portions for them to look at. My secretary could abstract the portions indicated and send it to the other person. I have since used the Multiplication Principle with experts to whom I have paid consulting fees for the consultation. In one case, I had a four-hour consultation with an expert from California who was only available by telephone while staying over the weekend in New York.

Although my time, plus his time and the telephone costs, came to a thousand dollars, when the information was passed around to other members of the group, we got ten thousand dollars in utility value from it.

6. A Trip Report Has Multiple Uses

At one firm where I was employed, it was necessary to make a written report before getting a settlement on any trip expenses. I found that this forced me to rethink the purposes of the trip and to recall what was obtained for the money and time spent. In some cases I went to see experts in other companies. I came across many good ideas which were useful to other members of my organization. I would obtain marketing information and production tips, and names of good suppliers, and so forth. *These tips were outside the scope of my work but I put them in my trip report and then abstracted those relevant portions and sent them on a voluntary basis to those who could use the information*

My experience with trip reporting indicates to me that even if you are not required to make out a trip report you would be well advised to do so for your own benefit. When you believe in the Time Awareness Principle (chapter 1), you want to know what contribution towards your purposes is obtained by any significant expenditure of your time.

7. The Multi-purpose Department Meeting has Many Benefits

Most managers and executives have periodic meetings with their teams in order to **review progress**. Information is passed down from above and reports are made from below.

Another purpose that might be served in department meetings is that of **cross-fertilization**. Independent specialists are not much inclined to tell each other about what they are doing, so the department meeting is a way of building inter-connections which help the department work as an integrated whole.

A department meeting can also be used to help (or hinder) **team building**. It can be a medium for joint problem-solving or for unproductive conflict and head-pecking. Now this is up to each individual manager, but one of the tools he has is to have a friendly coffee break or lunch with his staff.

Another purpose that may be served in a department meeting is the **development of the capabilities of the team**. Expertise from one member can be passed on to other by presentations. Outside speakers can bring new and challenging viewpoints to the managing group. While this kind of activity adds to the time of the meeting, not as much is required as for separate development activities.

8. Exemplary Discipline Can Save the Time Required for Reprimanding Everyone

There are times when the troops get a bit out of hand. For example, the advent of flexible hours has made it possible for more persons to cover-up when they arrive late or leave early. This sudden freedom sometimes requires additional corrective measures or people start slacking off. A few slackers tend to affect the morale of good workers and before you know it things are beginning to slip. Announcements and form letters will have a temporary effect. A more lasting effect would be to call in every individual to discuss the problem with them. However, this is probably more time consuming than the situation warrants. Can you use the Multiplication Principle here?

The administration of justice sometimes makes an example of a guilty person as a lesson to other would-be or minor offenders. This does not mean that a guilty person is picked at random for punishment. This would outrage the rest of the people especially if the "victim" was not a principal offender.

You can use the Multiplication Principle in a discipline problem if you don't use too heavy a hand. *Get the goods on a really guilty person and give that person enough of a reprimand so that other persons will know that you mean business.* Apply the discipline to the person who deserves it and the group will be with you and reinforce your effort. You will be using the Multiplication Principle because the effect on one will be felt by many. Moreover, if your move is in accord with the social norm of the group for being fair, then they will multiply your effort by their own comments to the truculent member.

ZERO IN ON THIS BREAKTHROUGH!

You multiply the use of one piece of work when you use the Multiplication Principle. Sometimes the work is useful again in exactly the same form. In other cases, the work may require additions or subtractions, but the bulk of it contributes to a time reduction on another task. Naturally, this does not apply to every activity and task because some are so unique that the results have no future use. On the other hand, when you are able to make it apply, the payoff can be tremendous because of the multiplication of the time saving. If you can find two uses for a piece of work, why not three, four or five? When you understand the principle and get better at it then you will achieve the higher levels of time saving that are possible. You will achieve a breakthrough in accomplishment.

You can see from the examples and techniques above that the Multiplication Principle is in fact being used in many situations already. The thing for you to do is to build your expertise in using the principle so that you can increase the multiplication number. **Love's jogger for multiplying the time saving—what other uses can I have for this piece of work?**

GUIDE TO MASTERY OF TIME

THE MULTIPLICATION PRINCIPLE

A task can sometimes be done in such a way that it contributes substantially to other tasks, thereby saving most of the time required for the other tasks. When the results of the first task have multiple uses, the time saved in the future is multiplied.

FIRST USE	SECOND USE	THIRD USE
(T)	◯	◯
[T]	▢	▢
(T)	▣	▣

Main Points

1. The performance level achieved by one task may have utility for the completion of another task.
2. The multiplication factor is not limited to two. It can be more.
3. Modular work is one tool for employing the Multiplication Principle.

Look Over Your Own Activities

Refer to the lists of tasks and activities in chapter 1, and to any augmentation of the list you have prepared. For each of these, ask yourself:

1. Can part of the performance level achieved be useful in the completion of this task when it occurs again? Mark: Yes; Maybe; or No.

2. Can work done in this task contribute to the performance required of another task? Yes or No. If yes, then insert the name of the task where the multiplication may occur.

3. For those tasks where the Multiplication Principle might apply, can modular work contribute to multiplication uses for it? Yes or No.

4. Make a plan of action for capitalizing on the Multiplication Principle.

5. Apply the Multiplication Principle to the work of your subordinates.

8 | How to Profit From Investing Your Time Wisely

KEY IDEA
Invest time and money in various ways to get
a regular dividend of extra time—using the
Investment Principle

THE REWARDS OF CAREFUL INVESTMENT

While living in the Caribbean, I became good friends
with a fellow manager who shared my interests in yachting.
He always seemed to have weeks of time for yachting. Even
as a landlubber, he had plenty of time for parties and other
social activities. One night, while anchored in the lee of a
sheltering island and relaxing with our evening libation, I
got up the nerve to ask him: "Percy, how is it you manage to
run a very active business and still have time for yachting
and parties?"

This is the substance of Percy's story. "In a nutshell,
Syd, I've invested a lot of time and money in getting my
business to the point where it is now. In the early years, a lot
of my savings were required to buy equipment and facilities

147

for the business, and I also put in a lot of hours building up the selling side of it. After a while, it got so that I could pay the bills and run the business by working only 16 hours a day! I began to worry. Although I was making money, I didn't really have much time to enjoy the things that money can buy. I needed time to do it. Fortunately for me, my father had taught me how to be systematic and organized, and how to lead a balanced life. First of all, I carefully examined all of the regular work that had to be done. Where it was possible, I made additional investments in equipment which could get the work done in less time. As the business was profitable, I could afford to do this and so began to save a little time. However, I found I couldn't be away from the business for extended periods unless I spent additional time in training people to run it for me. So I invested time in obtaining the right people and training them. I also invested time in setting up organized procedures that could be followed in my absence. After a while I found I could be away for two or three days at a time and never be missed. This gave my subordinates a chance to iron out the bugs in our procedures. Within one year, I had my hours down to a fairly regular working day, and I got up the courage to take a whole week at sea on my yacht without any contact with the business. When I got back, everything was running fine. My mind's cobwebs were cleared and I was able to take another look at improvements."

Percy's story is similar to that of many successful people I have met. The obvious point is that if you want to have time to "enjoy the fruits of your labours"—you must invest a little time to gain the freedom to take time off.

GET TIME DIVIDENDS BY USING THE INVESTMENT PRINCIPLE EXPLAINED IN THIS CHAPTER

If you are a serious reader of this book—you will get a lot more for your investment when you take a little extra time to learn and practice the principles made clear here. You are not likely to get there just by reading this chapter once over lightly. One of the big problems with time-harried people is that they can't seem to find time to start organizing themselves. This is a rationalization for not organizing time better. There may be unexpected payoffs in time management, but **the regular time dividend from systematic investment is what will pay off the most in the long run**. It's much more useful than rationalization.

BENEFITS FROM USING THE INVESTMENT PRINCIPLE ARE:

1. You will know where to make a time investment.
2. You will be able to get a steady dividend of extra time from certain kinds of time investments in routine activities.
3. You will be able to identify repeated activities where a resource investment will yield a time-saving payoff.

In this chapter you will learn about the Investment Principle and how to apply it to saving time. You will see how it is applied by the Jones family. They have a knack for using the Investment Principle without really knowing its explanation—but you will end up understanding the principle itself.

If you already grasp the principle, go directly to the "5 Techniques for Using the Investment Principle on the Job." Here, you will get practical tips as you see how Bob Jones used the Investment Principle again and again in his career. Then you can expand the use of the principle into more of your work and personal activities by using the "Guide to Time Mastery" at the end.

THE INVESTMENT PRINCIPLE

There are ways you can invest time or money in order to accomplish more of what you want to do. Like any investment, there is a chance you will lose if you don't invest it wisely. Now let's begin with a little theory on investments.

Time Investments with Leverage

In financial circles, when one controls a large amount of money with a small amount of investment, it is called financial leverage. For example, you can control a company with 51% of the stock, and this can be held by another company in which you own only 51% of its stock. Your net investment is then only 26% of the amount you control in the first company. So by cascading holding companies you might control a very large financial operation with an investment equivalent to that of a minor shareholder. This is leverage. On the other hand, if the bank requires assignment of all of your company's assets for lending you only a fifth of its value, then they are exercising leverage on you.

Suppose you are given a task which is going to take a year to complete. **A few days of planning at the beginning may save a month in the total project. This is a time investment with leverage**. Whenever the required time investment is much less than the normal time required of a task, then there is the possibility of a formidable dividend because of the high leverage exercised.

Another opportunity for leverage in time investment is when a routine task is repeated time and time again. Reorganization of the methods and procedures may require more time than doing the task once, but there is a small dividend each time the task is done again. There is a payback period in which the original time investment is paid back in small payments—then there is a clear time profit every time the task is done thereafter.

With time investments, the intent is to use **planning** or **methods improvements** so that the original time invested, TI, will be less than the total time that will ultimately be saved. The difference is the time dividend on your investment.

Time Saved Through Capital Investments

Machines are a means of transforming other forms of energy into accomplishments towards our purposes. A car is generally a good investment because the fast transportation is worth more than the cost of gasoline and depreciation on the car. A telephone is a good investment because it replaces running around to see people. Power tools extended our physical output just as the investment in a dictating equipment can increase our accomplishment in written words. Capital investments can help us accomplish more in the same time.

As human beings, we have poorer output devices than we have input devices. These can be made more efficient by the use of machines. *Our basic weakness as a human machine is that our output is slower than our input.* For example, we are barely able to talk at 200 words per minute but it is not difficult to learn to read at 600 words per minute. This is a one to three difference in rates of output and input.

Man's output devices are extended by machines which use energy to increase his power; transfer himself to another location; or transform output to another media. When you have many things to do and time has value (as outlined in chapter 1), you can profitably make capital investments in equipment which extends the power of your output.

THE INVESTMENT PRINCIPLE

If a long task or repeated activity is to be done—then invested time or invested resources may yield a dividend that exceeds the investment without any loss in the performance level.

INVESTMENTS OF T AND C		
T	C	T, C
T	C	T, C
T	C	T, C

HOW THE JONES USED THE INVESTMENT PRINCIPLE IN THE FAMILY BUSINESS

Looking Up Telephone Numbers

The Jones family moved to the west coast and started all over again in the family catering business. Soon the telephone memo board was decorated with pieces of paper with names and telephone numbers on them. Both covers of the telephone directory became scribbled with additional numbers as the quantity of telephone calls increased. However, the Jones family got used to it gradually. Looking up telephone numbers in the big directory, calling the operator for numbers, or asking each other for a number from their personal notebook, became the modus operandi and nobody thought that it could be any different. A printing company gave them a telephone number and address book as a gift. It was added to the pile of name and number recording places.

A minor family crisis led to the discovery that *telephone numbers should be organized*. When grandma died they had a lot of relatives to call and a lot of rearranging of catering personnel. "Never again," said mother (the real head of the business). A few weeks after the crisis she made orderly and systematic entries of all names, addresses and telephone numbers in the single book that they had been given. Before mother considered the task finished, *she had every member of the family transfer miscellaneous telephone numbers from their personal records into the master directory*. It took a little time, but after a few weeks of use most of the family saw the value in keeping the master directory up to date for both business and personal contacts.

This is *an example of changing the method on a repeated activity*. Time must be invested in the beginning— but it all gets paid back with additional dividends eventually.

Investing in a Redecorating Plan

When the time came for the Jones family to have their silver wedding anniversary, business was good and father promised that the house could be decorated as an anniversary present. With a house full of teenagers who were coming and going for band practices, pajama parties, and studying for exams, mother could see such a hassle developing that the children might sue for divorce—not to mention the need to keep the catering equipment moving freely in and out of the garage. She had about six months to get the thing done before the anniversary celebration.

After 25 years of homemaking and working in their catering business, mother was a past master of the intuitive use of the Addition Principle, Multiplication Principle, Alternatives Principle, and Maximum Utility Principle, although she could not make speeches about them. She could also use the Investment Principle. During one quiet morning *she invested time to plan out the redecorating in detail.* To run the business, they needed to invest in a telephone equipped van which would serve as a mobile office and save time. That night she submitted the plan to the family for revision and review. *With their participation in the final planning, she obtained their cooperation* in rescheduling certain things and sold them on the new van idea. The whole decorating program finally got off the ground and flew without any crash landings.

With the Investment Principle, you should be aware that:

1. Time can be invested with a profit if more time is to be saved later on.
2. You can invest a little money in equipment that will be worth it in the time saved.

FIVE TECHNIQUES FOR USING THE INVESTMENT PRINCIPLE ON THE JOB

1. Cutting Down on Telephone Interruptions

Bob J. was a hard working specialist in a California electronics firm who had demonstrated a capacity for getting things done. After ten years with his organization he was promoted to the management level. He now had 25 people who reported to him through four supervisors. Bob found that he had to shift gears and become a delegator instead of a doer. He did his best to delegate the work to his four supervisors, but one problem remained—though Bob was willing to delegate his responsibilities, the people with whom he had worked for years were not about to drop their direct contact with him.

Bob noticed that he got a lot of calls for action on problems and this kept him busy calling in the supervisors to get action started and follow up on previous problems. Occasionally, he would sit down and try and do some long-range planning, but before long he would be interrupted by a call from one of his buddies who wanted some action. At times, Bob felt like telling them to shove off and leave him alone, but he realized that he needed to be willing to help his co-managers with their problems.

As far as he was concerned, the calls could go directly to his supervisors and he would be happy for them to only inform him about unusual ones. Still, he could not tell his callers that he was too busy and they should call his supervisors. It would have to be more subtle than that—and would require a little time investment from him.

WHAT BOB DID TO CUT DOWN ON TELEPHONE INTERRUPTIONS.

> When someone called about a problem he first inquired about the essential details. After promising to look after it, he sat back to consider whether he should do it himself or refer it to a subordinate. In many cases he referred it to a subordinate and told the subordinate to call back the other party with the answer. This let his colleagues know where the action was and indicated to them that he did not mind them talking with his supervisors.

After a while most of his colleagues found that they saved time by going directly to Bob's supervisors. Moreover, *Bob never indicated any irritation with the fact that they bypassed him.*

After six months of subtly educating his routine callers

and helping his supervisors overcome protocol difficulties, Bob found that his "problem solving" telephone calls had been reduced substantially and he had more time for planning. His time investment in "educating" his callers had paid off.

2. The Weekly Managers' Reports

Hard work, a balanced family life, and willingness to be flexible, had paid off when Norton P. J. was promoted to the executive suite of a New York firm. His friends thought he had it made. The euphoria lasted for about one year and then Norton found that he was under tremendous time pressures. As an executive he travelled a lot more and attended a lot more high level meetings. Yet he felt he had to keep informed on what his subordinate managers were doing. He scheduled regular weekly meetings with each one of them separately. This was done in informal fashion. They sat in comfortable chairs around a small coffee table and a secretary served them fresh coffee. Norton liked the informal and unstructured approach. Most of his managers had organized minds and were able to cover the important things in an informal manner. It also gave his managers a chance to sound him out on new ideas.

When Norton realized that he was spending about ten hours a week on this activity, he remembered that a person could read at a rate which is three times as fast as that at which they could listen—because of the difference in reading rates and speaking rates. When he thought of this his first impulse was to ask his managers to make out weekly reports for him to read. Again, he thought back to the days when he used to do that and about how many times he had drafted and revised the weekly reports which went upstairs. It had taken a lot of time and he had much preferred an informal discussion of progress with his executive.

There had to be a way, and Norton pondered the problem until a solution came to him in a flash one day. He chanced to see one of his managers dictating some notes into a pocket-sized tape recorder. This, he thought would enable the managers to talk to him in a manner similar to the face-to-face conversations he had with them. They could talk from the shoulder, so to speak. However, if he listened to the tapes he would spend just as much time as he would listening to the person and he would not be able to interrupt and ask questions. He discussed his thoughts with some of the managers and this is what they came up with:

WHAT NORTON DID TO SAVE TIME
ON WEEKLY REPORTS

1. They all invested in dictating systems which included a small pocket-sized tape recorder. Each manager was allowed a maximum 30 minutes of dictation time, with a target of 15 minutes. However, they did not just ramble on into the tape recorder—they were structured reports. Each manager made a heading outline of his topics and marked those which were in his estimation the most important for his executive to read. The marked outline and the tape were sent to the executive's secretary who transcribed all of the tapes. This allowed them to be very confidential, but if the managers wanted to have transcriptions done by their own secretaries, this was acceptable too.

2. Now, for the meeting part. The executive scheduled 15 minutes with each of his managers, but prior to each meeting he looked at the outline and scanned the transcriptions. He marked those parts he had questions on and had it ready when his manager came to see him. In a few minutes they could cover the highlights and take time to review and discuss some of the items which required joint problem solving. The executive found that the total time devoted to his managers' weekly progress reports was cut in half.

It took a little time for his managers to get used to the new system, but after a while they reported that they also were saving time. Some of them passed the idea down the line for use with their supervisors.

3. Referable Telephone Calls

As an executive, Norton P. J. found he was more and more the target for unsolicited phone calls which would interrupt him in the middle of some of his planning periods. He needed time to think. Some unsolicited calls could not be turned aside through screening by his secretary—because an irate customer might have a connection with the Board of Directors. Being "too busy" or "in conference" was not the best solution. Since most of his work was delegated anyway, he could ultimately refer each caller to one of his managers. He recalled the days when he was a manager and how he had educated his regular callers to go to his subordinates—but you cannot educate a person who calls infrequently. He could, however, educate his secretary and this is what he did.

WHAT NORTON DID TO SAVE TIME ON REFERABLE CALLS

If he was tied up, he instructed his secretary to say as much, and to offer to get someone else to help the caller. He prepared his secretary for this by making up a list of the duties and responsibilities of each of the managers, and by having the managers agree that they would handle these calls. Norton found that many of his callers could be satisfied by referral to another authority as long as they got prompt action. The callers were invited to call back if they did not get satisfaction.

What worried Norton about this technique was the tendency of his secretary to hand out these delegations with a heavy hand, as if she was acting with his full authority. He told her never to refer a call with the inference that it was "his wish" that action be taken immediately—priority was up to the manager. Each referred caller was to be treated as if they had called the manager directly. If it was in their scope of authority, they would handle it; if not, they would refer it just as he had done.

He monitored his system for a few months to iron out the wrinkles and according to the records kept by his secretary, about 50 percent of the unsolicited telephone calls were referable. After a while she developed a sense of discretion in referring calls and acquired tact in dealing with callers. Nevertheless, he made sure that he was always accessible if a caller really needed him.

4. Digging into New Problems with the Help of a Research Assistant

As an executive of a Boston insurance company, Kevin E. found that he was often given special problems to handle. If a problem didn't fit clearly into any of the responsibilities of the executives, the top banana frequently gave it to him. He soon found out that any new type of problem required a bit of research. His regular organization was not equipped to handle one-time tasks which involved exploring a new territory.

Kevin was getting the reputation for handling special assignments well, but it was eating into the time he needed for his regular management, and for living a balanced family life. Why should he, an executive responsible for 4,000 other persons, be working weekends doing library research on some new situation? The time had come for him to invest some of the company resources in doing this kind of job for him. *He employed a research assistant who had the ability to dig up facts on new situations.* The investment in this human resource paid off even more in the future when the organization found it had a lot of new government regulations to contend with. Kevin took care that his research assistant did not usurp his authority and play the role of an assistant executive. Because he had a research assistant, he actually had more time to deal directly with the people who needed to see him personally.

5. *Personal Style at Meetings*

As the chief architect of a Montreal construction firm, Pierre Q. did not have much time to think about the development of his subordinates. One of his managers had risen through his technical expertise primarily, but was something of a liability at group meetings. Not that this person didn't try, but he was not good at self-expression or at running his own meetings.

At lunch one day with the manager, Pierre told him about his own experience as a new manager some years ago. He had realized that he had a lot to learn about the conduct of meetings so he had gone to night school to learn the rudiments of public speaking and the conduct of meetings. He had learned about Robert's Rules of Order and other formalities. He had learned to stand up and be heared without getting nervous, especially after reducing his French accent. In Pierre's view his time investment in self-development had contributed to his getting ahead in management.

The manager got the message and *went to night school to learn about meetings and style.* In three months, Pierre noticed a change in his style, and gave him encouraging praise. In one year the problem was solved and Pierre thought that *the time that he himself had invested in giving subtle encouragement had paid off well.*

USING THE INVESTMENT PRINCIPLE
TO GAIN TIME

To use the investment principle you must have the courage to take some time now and invest it for the payoffs later on. It's like investing money. A little bit invested early in life will pay off in big dividends later on. It often appears wise to make an investment when you can least afford it. That is the paradox of time investment. When you are already very busy, you realize that you must invest some extra time in order to get more free time later on!

There are plenty of opportunities for investing your time to save time. There are also opportunities for investing in additional resources to save time, such as: equipment that speeds up your output; hiring of additional people; the development of human resources available to you; and the development of your own resource capability by lifelong education.

As illustrated in the examples and techniques above, there are many places in work life and private life to apply the investment principle. It applies especially well to routine activities in which the the payback is over a long period. Once you understand the principle you can extend it into intermittent activities where the payoff is not so big or certain, but is worthwhile nevertheless.

GUIDE TO TIME MASTERY

THE INVESTMENT PRINCIPLE

If a long task or repeated activity is to be done—then invested time or invested resources may yield a dividend that exceeds the investment without any loss in the performance level.

INVESTMENTS OF T AND C		
T	C	T , C
T	C	T , C
T	C	T , C

Main Points

1. You get a regular dividend from time invested in improving the method and procedure of doing a routine task.

2. You get a one-time payoff by planning ahead in a major new task.

3. Self-development of your own resources is good investment.

4. You can invest money in equipment and devices that improve your output.

5. You can invest time and money to get a dividend from the difference in the reading and speaking rates of people.

Guidelines

1. Develop a list of routine activities such as that shown in chapter 1 (or use copies made earlier). For each one of these make a judgment and answer .. Yes; Maybe; or No . . . to the following question for each activity. **"Can the method or equipment be changed to reduce the time required?"** Then go to work on the "yes" ones. Do some investing so that you can get the time dividend.

2. What abilities do you need to accomplish more? This really breaks down into two areas: (a) work life, (b) personal life. Make a list of needed abilities. You should realize that development of your abilities allows you to accomplish more in the same time (or to accomplish the same in less time). For example, you may have learned to compose letters in a laborious fashion, but eventually improved your skill so that you can now dash them off quickly.

   Are there skills and know-how that you could acquire that would enable you to accomplish more?

From your list of needed abilities, pick out one which is important but has room for improvement. Make a plan to invest a little time in developing that skill or knowhow by self study, night school, or coaching.

3. The human being is more limited in output devices than in input devices. For example, you can read at least three times as fast as you can speak. The eyes have tremendous capacity for input because, as they say, "A picture is worth a thousand words." The following is a small catalogue of devices that man uses to extend his input or output capacity. Are any of these of value to you?

DEVICES TO EXTEND YOUR CAPACITY

Physical Strength	*Spoken Words*	*Written Words*	*Body Language*
—cars	—message condensing secretary	—voice recorder and transcriber	—closed-circuit TV
—power tools	—portable tape recorder	—shorthand	—video tape recorder
—motors	—large audience	—cryptic short forms in writing	—film
—amplifiers of strength (like power steering	—loudspeaker	—camera (a picture is worth a thousand words)	
—push-button controls	—telephone		
	—2-way radio		

4. Review the list of investment ideas in the appendix, "Time-Saving Equipment, Devices and Forms," and make plans to invest resources where it can count.

9 | Time-Saving Techniques For Storing and Retrieving Information

KEY IDEA
Time can be saved on locating information
when it is stored with organized clues—
using the Retrieval Principle

ONCE FILED, HOW DO I FIND IT?

Have you ever misplaced a business letter? Well, I have. More than once. One particular lost letter upset me quite a bit—but it taught me a lesson.

A few years ago I needed to have a copy of an important letter which concerned a legal-technical matter. It was wanted by my boss for an executive meeting on the next morning. It put me in a cold sweat because if I did not find it quickly, my boss and I would appear incompetent.

My new secretary had looked for an hour before leaving for the day. She had done her best. If only Nancy, my previous secretary, had still been there. She could find anything by memory but I never did find out how she filed things. I looked in the files by sender's name, company name, my name, date sent and date received (as much as I could recall them). I checked my in-basket and my follow-up basket.

Three times. I never did find it. After a week we got another copy from the sender. In the meantime, I was fortunate enough to get by with a memo which stated my recollection of the contents.

After that incident, I decided to have files and records that were indexed so that anyone could use them. Which I did. Now, years later, I understand better how the human mind works. Certain kinds of clues are best for retrieving anything we store in our minds or files. From this I have developed the Retrieval Principle. I use it now for organizing office files or for computerized information retrieval systems. It's simple and it works. I will explain it to you in this chapter.

HOW YOU WILL BENEFIT FROM USING THE RETRIEVAL PRINCIPLE

The above situation was a problem of information retrieval which was wasteful of time and money. When you understand the Retrieval Principle, which you will learn about in this chapter, you will use the best way to store information in the first place. Your mind is a vast treasury of information, but like Captain Kidd's buried gold, you need a map to get there.

BENEFITS OF USING THE RETRIEVAL PRINCIPLE ARE:

1. You will save time in finding stored information because the Retrieval Principle will have guided you into the best file organization for storing the information.

2. You will save time in learning new things because you will store them in your mind in the order and manner of recall.

3. You will be more effective in written communications because you will understand how the receiver wants the information organized.

4. You will be more effective in giving instructions because you will understand how the other person retrieves them.

To better understand the Retrieval Principle you should scan the three following everyday examples to get a clear idea of what the principle implies. If you already understand the principle quite well, then go directly to the specific techniques. There are six smart ways to use the Retrieval Principle—in filing; in project workbooks; in special reports; in giving special instructions; in agendas; and in minutes of meetings.

Then it would be appropriate for you to apply the principle itself to your own specific activities. This comes under the section, "Guide to Time Mastery".

THE RETRIEVAL PRINCIPLE

The capacity of a human mind to store information is enormous. There isn't a computer memory bank yet built that can store as much as the mind of a single person. Consider the fact that in one lifetime you read hundreds of books and thousands of pages of newspapers. You write all kinds of exercises at school, numerous letters in business, and so forth. In addition to that, you have the input to your eyes from movies, television, and all of the other things you see. It appears to us that most of this information goes in and is lost, but the facts are otherwise. For example, neurosurgeons have electrically stimulated the brain and enabled people to recall in minute detail the writings and conversations experienced in their childhood. A great neurologist, Wilder Penfield, has stated that everything that a person is conscious of in every waking moment is permanently recorded in the brain. You know yourself that you can have vivid dreams of events that took place many years ago, but if you tried to recall them consciously, you would probably draw a blank.

We need some organized way in which to get access to the vast amount of information stored in our brain. In quiz games it is not unusual for the respondent to say, "Give me a clue." *A clue seems to be able to unlock a whole area of memory which is not otherwise accessible.* A person may need a few more clues until he finally pinpoints the exact information that was in his mind all along.

The reason we need clues is that the conscious mind can only review a limited amount of stored memory at a time. If all the facts of our life's existence suddenly came into our conscious mind, we would be overwhelmed and not able to make any sense of it. The vast amount of storage in the human brain is attached to a very slow output device, whether it be the conscious thinking mind or the speaking voice. Because of this, we need some devices such as clues, leads, or structured thought which enable us to get to that part of the memory which is important to us at a given point in time.

There are various ways of accessing the brain which are in common use. People who teach a second language to others know that it is almost a waste of time to have them learn words as if they were to become a dictionary. Language is much better learned by phrases which are associated within a specific context. In other words, a set of phrases pertaining to a restaurant is more easily learned than a dictionary of all terms used in a restaurant. This is why a phrase book is so much more useful than a dictionary to the traveller who is learning a new language. A phrase book has the other language ordered or arranged according to the use to which it will be put. Within each category, for example, restaurant, the phrases are *arranged in the order of use*. So under restaurant phrases you would find, first of all, asking for the menu, and last of all asking for the bill.

A bus schedule is a good example of a well organized information retrieval system. First the schedules are divided into air, train and bus; then into east, west, north and south. You get the right booklet and then you find the schedule. It is arranged with emphasis on the start time and the end time. They are very convenient for you to use. Imagine, if you will, the train schedule which is organized by the numbers of the locomotives which pull them. It would be very difficult to retrieve the traveller's information from it. So whether it be bus, train, or air schedules, or learning to recall a new language, the common practice has evolved to a *user-oriented organization which assists the retrieval of useful information*.

Now, let's put these ideas together. The mind can store a lot but requires a retrieval technique to get at the important stuff. At the same time, society has found that retrieval systems which are organized for the users' benefit are the most readily understood. These facts of life strongly support the concept that information can best be stored for re-use if the clues are user-oriented. This is the essence of the Retrieval Principle.

If the performance, P, of an activity or task depends primarily on the use of stored information, then P will never be perfect because it is not feasible to recover more than a fraction of the original information which was stored in our mind, or the minds of persons working on the task. When we establish the performance level of such a task beforehand, and allocate resources, C, to the project, then both P and C are fixed. The time, T, is the variable that can be reduced by employing a retrieval system which takes the shortest amount of time to get an adequate level of information. Information should be retrieved in the order of use. For this to happen, the information should first be stored with clues, guides, and indices which are user-oriented.

THE RETRIEVAL PRINCIPLE

Where the performance, P, of an activity depends primarily on the use of stored information, the time, T, will be least when the information was first stored with user-oriented clues.

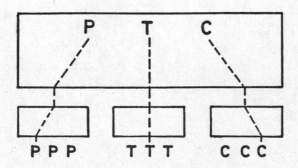

EVERYDAY EXAMPLES OF USING THE
RETRIEVAL PRINCIPLE

Finding Your Car in a Parking Lot

James D. was a salesman whose business often took him
into the center of large eastern cities. He was always using
strange parking lots. The ones that gave him the most trouble were the large multiple-story parking buildings. It was
not that he couldn't find the entrance; it was not that he
couldn't find a place to park; his problem was that he often
couldn't find his car when he wanted to leave.

While parking his car, his mind was on the customer he
was about to see. He would turn into the first parking space
he could find and make his way to the elevator. Then a
couple of hours later he would return to the building and try
to remember on which floor his car was. Even if he remembered the floor, he would not be sure which elevator shaft he
was to take. Once off the elevator, he would look around for
his ordinary-looking Ford, and make many false discoveries
before finding his own. Once he had a memory blank-out
and walked all of a seven-story spiral before he found his
car. That did it! There had to be a better way. James was no
dummy so he started marking his parking ticket with the
floor number. This worked pretty well until the day he left
his parking ticket in the car. Everybody makes a few mis-
takes.

One day he was late for an appointment because of having to look for his car and blurted out the unhappy truth to
his customer when excusing himself for being late. The customer laughed and said that he understood because he had
had this problem many times in the past. He had once taken
his wife to the opera and spent thirty minutes afterwards
trying to find his car. It was such a dumb thing to do he decided he needed additional memory joggers. So now when
he parks his car he takes as many "clues" as he can about his
whereabouts. First there is the floor and bay number. But as
he may forget those, he makes a mental note of any codes on

the elevator shaft that he's using; takes note of any unusual cars parked in his vicinity; and tries to orient himself with respect to the down ramp. *With many clues he is always able to recall the location of his car* without a lot of fooling around. James D. took the hint and now notes several clues so that he is certain to find his car again.

The point of this example is that clues are necessary. The more the better.

Tool Storage in the Garage Can Be a Handyman's Delight

Tony A. was a man who liked to tinker with cars and work on his hobbies. He had acquired quite a collection of tools and gadgets and they were piled one on top of the other in his garage. He also stored his garden equipment in there. Tony liked to keep things tidy, so he decided to cover one wall with pegboard and put as many of the tools as he could on the wall. He had seen one of these at night school, and he noticed that all of the wrenches were in one place, all of the screwdrivers in another and all the saws in another, and so forth. It sure did look good.

However, our Tony had an intuitive feeling for the Retrieval Principle and he felt that *since the pegboard tool rack was for his benefit alone, then he should arrange it in the way that suited him and not worry too much about its orderly appearance.* If he used a tool often, it should be close to where he used it. So what Tony did was to put most of his woodworking tools over the work-bench and put most of his car tools near the engine end of the car. He reasoned that the garden tools should go close to the door, along with miscellaneous shovels and brushes because they were required outside of the garage.

What Tony liked about the pegboard was that he could shift his tool positions around as he saw his needs changing. When he got another tool he could put it up on the wall, and if space was lacking he could probably take down something that was not much in use anymore. Admittedly, Tony didn't have the neatest, most beautiful tool rack in the neighborhood but it did serve his purposes very well. It also settled a longstanding argument between him and his teen-age sons. They were using the garage for fixing up their hot-rods and leaving the tools all over the place. Now Tony could tell at a glance whether the tools were in place and so could his sons. They now have a modus operandi that promotes cooperation instead of conflict.

The point of this example is that things are easier to retrieve if arranged in the order in which they will be used, whether tools or information.

Serving Club Members with an Organized Membership List

The citizens of a small but affluent industrial town in Kentucky organized a golf and country club. Through subscriptions and loans they built a fine clubhouse facility and over the years were able to extend it to include a swimming pool and tennis courts.

When the membership reached four hundred, the administrative problems got a bit out of hand. Janice D. was asked by the executive committee to look after the membership records. Because of family membership and club affiliations, the membership mailing list had grown to about a thousand names. It was decided to go from a manual addressing procedure to one of the mechanized systems. Janice had to decide which was the best system.

If addresses were put on metal labels, they could be stored in alphabetical order and this would be very convenient for changing addresses. Janice recognized that the club now had many activities which involved different sub-groups of members. She wondered if it would be possible to sort out the mailing list by interest groups so they could plan events and inform only interested members about them. For example, there would be the group that identify themselves as golfers; and those interested in tennis; and those social members who go to all the dances; and others who would come to meetings with a special guest speaker. If, at membership renewal time, members gave a profile of their interests, then they could be asked to join in the planning of special group activities. This meant that they could be filed by interest groups, although there would be some names that would appear in more than one group. Then each interest group could be run off as a list to let other members of the group know who's who. The committee chairman could also use the special list for obtaining volunteers.

Janice found that the mailing list could go on special key-sort cards which could be sorted out according to interest codes which were punched on the edge of the cards. However, it happened that Janice's son was a computer programmer and sold her on the idea of putting the membership list on a computer. Then she would be able to get all kinds of sortings. Updates could be easily made by filling out a card which would be sent for keypunching and entering into the computer prior to the next run. All this service was performed by a general data processing firm. Address labels which could be easily stuck onto envelopes were also available from the computer run-off. Her son volunteered to get the system working, thus saving a startup cost of a thousand dollars. Once it was going the monthly charges were under $25, and Janice figured that was a good buy, especially since the membership could now double and the system could still handle it.

The point of this example is that it pays to look ahead and anticipate future uses of any information storage system, be it membership list or company records.

Now that you have read the Retrieval Principle and looked at three everyday examples of its use, examine the specific uses below for ideas to put to use at work.

SIX SMART WAYS TO USE THE RETRIEVAL PRINCIPLE

1. *How to Reorganize a Filing System*

Ben D. was an engineer who was recently promoted from supervisor to manager in a middlesized manufacturing concern in the west. While he was supervisor, his boss's secretary had kept the master files while he had kept his own copies filed by date. Even after he acquired his own secretary, they continued to use the filing system that he had previously developed for his own use. It was very simple. However, as the years went on and the number of letters increased in frequency, it was necessary to take another look. He was frequently irritated by the time taken to retrieve a letter when he didn't know at least the approximate date of its being received or sent. To be out by a month was to have someone look through two inches or more of letters.

Ben knew that something should be done about it because on TV he saw a secretary get a copy of her boss's letter in a minute. Eventually he would get one of those microfilm systems himself, but for the time being his needs did not warrant that kind of capital investment.

He asked his secretary for advice. She thought that she could save time if his letters were filed alphabetically by the addressee's name, even though he may just be a flunkie in a big corporation. Filing alphabetically by the addressee's affiliation was another possibility, especially since a lot of correspondence went to a few suppliers. Ben was inclined to think there was a better way so he put it on the back burner for a few weeks.

Shortly after apologizing to his boss for taking an hour to retrieve a certain letter in which the vendor had promised early delivery, Ben decided it was time to develop something else. Imagine that you are able to tune in on Ben's thoughts as he worked it out. It probably went something like this: "How am I going to use this information? For one thing, I like to have all matters pertaining to each project in one folder or book so that I can take that project file with me to the meeting. That is also the way I review the work of the various engineers who report to me. At the same time, it would be nice to have a file of each of our major vendors so that I could check on any past promises or commitments that we or they made. Then it seems to me I need to have some way of retrieving letters from other members of my own organization. It wouldn't be enough just to file them under the company name because there would be too many of them. That file should be split down into the names of the senders because I know all of those persons quite well. I would like to be able to say to my secretary, 'Give me the file of letters from Joe Billings.' If Joe was on the telephone I would like that file to be instantly available. Then there's the matter of internal reports. I get a lot of these and they should be filed under our company name, but not under the name of the sender, because all of one kind of report should be kept together in a file. Then I can take it with me to a meeting."

Ben thought about a matrix filing system in which each letter would have a copy filed under the sender's company affiliation, by the project, and by the date. It would mean making two copies of every letter received and although the secretary could carry out these instructions it would eventually amount to a lot of paperwork. He was not unaware that the true cost of making a copy is far in excess of the actual charge for making a copy on the machine. It seemed to him that there should be a decision-making function which would select out certain letters for multiple filing, and the others would go into a standard file. What Ben finally came up with was this procedure, which he dictated as instructions to his secretary and then discussed with her.

EXAMPLE OF A FILE REORGANIZATION

1. All letters sent by or to me are to be in a separate file from those of other members of my department. These are to be confidential. Mark the file accordingly.

2. All major suppliers and customers with whom I deal are to have separate file folders which are to be kept in alphabetical order. Other letters are to be collected in folders marked with the first letter of the sender's affiliation.

3. Within each file folder the letters are to be filed towards the front by the sender's date.

4. A new file cabinet is to be set aside for project files. In it are to be the projects by sequential numbers as they are initiated. The folders are to be titled with the project name as well. On my desk I am to have a small card on which the names and project numbers are listed.

5. When a letter is to be cross-filed in a project file, I will indicate the project number on the upper right-hand corner. For example, +34 will indicate an additional copy to be put in project file #34. The project files are to be internally organized by sections which will be called correspondence; specification; schedules; cost and time records; and miscellaneous. At the front of the correspondence section will be a colored sheet of paper which will be used to note the file location of more complicated letters or reports which will not be duplicated for this file. When such a letter or report crosses my desk, I will mark it +34N, the N indicating the notation in the project folder #34.

6. When a project is completed, the file is to be removed from the main drawer and kept in numerical sequence in a holding file drawer. The active projects will not be loaned without a notation in the file as to their whereabouts.

7. All internal correspondence is to be under the company name in a section which is to be subdivided by the alphabetized surnames of the persons with whom I correspond.

8. As for third party copies of letters that I receive, I will scan these and either discard them or mark them for filing in one of the files.

9. Within the company file section will be a section called "Internal Reports" and these are to be in separate folders indexed alphabetically by the title of the report.

10. I am to have a brief list of all file names and numbers which can be posted on the wall near my desk.

11. All files are to be considered active for the current year and the past two years. All material older than that is to be sent to the archive files until five years old at which time the legal unit is to be asked for advice on what to keep.

Ben is a very organized person now. He not only saves himself time by a user-oriented filing and retrieval system, but his whole unit is disciplined by the procedure.

2. *Portable Project Workbooks Save Me Time*

In my type of work, which is mainly management consulting, each contract is considered to be a separate project. It is important for me to have the records for that contract with me when I am working on the client's premises, or in my office, or working while travelling.

When a new contract is initiated, I acquire a high-quality, three-ring notebook which has storage pockets in the covers. I like to start a new color for each active contract so there is less chance of mixing them up. The book is well labelled as to its ownership, with addresses and telephone numbers in case it is misplaced. So far I have not lost one of these project books, but in any case, I do have a backup set of records in the main office. Any important work which I carry around with me is usually copied and filed before I take irreplaceable originals with me.

Each project workbook has a set of index dividers which are made up especially for that project. While there is some commonality, I find that each project is different and requires its own unique set of labels. However I do find that I can start up with divisions for: correspondence; directory of personnel; a task list; schedules; and, at the back, a miscellaneous paper and forms section.

If you use a project notebook, you may not want to

punch holes in the originals you are keeping there. That's what the pockets in the covers are for. If you do not have these you can purchase an insert which will hold additional papers without punching holes in them.

Within any section, it is my preference to file to the front so that when I open that section the most recent work is immediately in front of me. One of my colleagues prefers to do it the other way, but that doesn't matter because each of us uses his own workbook. **The point to be made is that our project workbooks are definitely user-oriented with unique index clues which make it easy for us to retrieve** information or work sheets in the minimum amount of time.

3. User-oriented Reports Accomplish More

Many well organized reports are based on a logical development of facts which lead up to the major conclusion or point to be made. This is a form of inductive reasoning and is quite appropriate for persuading a captive audience to do thus and so.

Another form of report organization is that learned at school by engineers and scientists of all types. Generally it starts with a hypothesis which is followed by a description of the experimental procedure. Then the experimental results are presented and discussed. Finally a conclusion is made about the truth of the hypothesis. It is all very logical. The scientist would probably not have it any other way.

Managers and executives in non-scientific operations are not impressed by a report which is so logically developed. One may impress another scientist by such a report, but for communicating upwards in an organization they are almost useless—unless an executive manager has learned to first go to the end of the report to find the conclusion, because that is where the 'meat' is to be found. Some authors recommend that business reports be in the reverse order of scientific reports: that is, **the conclusion comes at the beginning instead of at the end.** This is a strong orientation to the user and is an application of the Retrieval Principle.

When you finally sit down to make up a special report which covers a considerable amount of preceding work, it is only natural that you think chronologically of the events. So you are likely to report this in abbreviated form: "Well, first we did this and then we tried this other thing. After a while we found that worked and thus and so . . . Finally, after exhaustively going through all these trials we hit upon the idea of . . . And in conclusion let me say . . ."

The Index of a Chronologically Organized Report Might Look Like This:

Origin of problem
History of problem
Experimental methodology
Description and result of trial solution A
Description and result of trial solution B
Description and result of trial solution C
The solution chosen
Recommendations for further study
Bibliography

If this kind of report is sent upstairs, it is fortunate if it has an index, because the reader may go to the important part about the solution chosen instead of setting the whole thing aside until some indefinite future date. I have heard people who sent up elaborate reports complaining that they were never read. Some of the fault lies with the sender. Let me reorganize the general report and suggest a better order of contents:

A User-Oriented Organization of a Report

Executive summary
Major finding
Immediate action required
Appendix I—Details of recommended solution
Appendix II—Other solutions investigated
Appendix III—Experimental methodology
Appendix IV—Annotated selected bibliography

Naturally, every special report will require its own index. The principle here is that the users can best be served by being able to retrieve the essential information without a waste of time. Invest a little extra time in organizing the report for the user's benefit and more of it will be read and understood.

Another rule of thumb about reports that go upstairs is that: *the bigger the report, the less chance it will be read and understood.* It takes an effort to boil down a report into a lucid and clearly understood summary which is decision and action oriented. Yet the effort is usually quite small in comparison with the total time spent gathering the information and organizing it for the report, and it ensures that that time will not be wasted. Pick a frame of reference based upon the Retrieval Principle and you will have successful reports.

4. Save Time on Diagrams by Using Modular Instructions to Your Secretary

For reporting to a high level, you may very well reverse the order of reporting so that the conclusion comes first. On the other hand, if you are giving instructions for having some work done for you, you should not reverse the order. The Retrieval Principle requires you to communicate so that the user can retrieve with the greatest ease; that is, in the order of use, whatever it may be. The Retrieval Principle applies to giving special instructions—make sure there are ample clues in your instructions so that the person can recall the instructions in more than one manner. Let me give you an example.

Suppose you are giving your secretary instructions on making up a diagram for one of your reports. This kind of work is so tricky that you may prefer to do it yourself. However, you can save time by instructing your secretary carefully to do work with a pencil and pen. For this she was not originally trained but she will soon derive a sense of accomplishment from making diagrams if she is instructed correctly.

What you should do is think out your instructions in the form of independent modules so that these can be additional clues for retrieval by the listener. For example, the four main modules in drawing a flow chart are: to sketch; type; ink; and put on arrowheads. Just imagine that you are listening in on me as I give instructions to my secretary:

SKETCH MODULE

"Mary, I would like you to do the diagrams for this report. They are called flowcharts and about 50 percent of the work is typing. If you can also draw in the lines you will be a more valuable secretary to me. Have you done any of these before? No. Well, *let me show you* how I think you should do it. First, take a clear sheet of paper like this and *sketch* in the blocks in pencil, just as I am doing here. You can *erase*, and shift the blocks around after you have typed in the pencilled blocks." (The verbal clues are sketch, erase, and the visual clue is from my sketch.)

TYPE MODULE

"The next thing that you should do is *type* in the headings in capital letters and see how they *fit* in your boxes. Don't expect it to be perfect the first time. You should plan to lay another piece of paper over your first typed one and sketch the boxes again with better sizes and arrangements. Note how I leave spaces between the boxes for insertion of the *arrows* which you will do later. I think the second time around you will have the headings and the boxes well organized for space. Look here, if I put the letters in this box, I want to avoid hyphenating the word 'inspection.' Therefore I must start another line or lengthen the first line. You see? O.K. Shall we go on?"

INK MODULE

"Now comes the part which is probably new to you. I spent years learning to draw in *ink* and I don't suppose this is going to come easy to you. However, I have here a special ball point pen that flows very freely with black ink. You will notice that there is a little *notch* in the plastic material of your typing window. You can put the pen in there and *turn the roller* around and you will get a *vertical* line. *See how I do it*? If you push the spacer bar you will get a *horizontal* line. The boxes will be perfectly square. I prefer the ink to the typewriter underline because it gives a smooth line. You can *check the location and size with a pencil first* and then do them in ink on your typewriter. Here, put this sheet that I have drawn in your typewriter and draw the horizontal and vertical lines around this box . . .good. With a little *practice* you can get the lines to touch exactly . . . .if they don't, just use a little bit of white-out and they will look fine in the final report because we will be using copies anyway." (The verbal clues are *roller*, *pen*, *horizontal*, *vertical* and so forth. There are recall clues through the secretary's hands. When she picks up the pen she will probably remember exactly where to place it on the typewriter.)

ARROWHEAD MODULE

"Now let's do some arrowheads. It took me a long time to learn how to do these in drafting class so I'm going to show you two neat ways to do it without a lot of practice. Firstly, you can use this *plastic overlay* without a cutout in it. You can draw a nice *triangular arrowhead* where it touches the box and you can draw the arrow line up to the head. Try one . . .O.K. I think you will need practice with that. In the meantime obtain a set of arrows on a letter transfer sheet and you can just rub them into place. I prefer that you use the open arrowheads rather than the solid ones because the copy machine doesn't work well on solid ones. Try putting the arrows on the diagram.

So you see, it won't be difficult to learn if you do it in the order that I have told you: sketch them; type in the headings; ink in the boxes; and then put on the arrowheads." (Reinforcing the major clues.)

5. *Personalize an Advance Meeting Agenda and Save Everyone Time*

When you call a meeting with sufficient advance notice, you can save time during the meeting by giving the participants an opportunity to prepare their part in advance. It's a good idea to send out an agenda and expect people to come prepared. However, don't expect that the mere presence of a line-by-line list of agenda items will suffice to do that. Many people will be content to scan through and hope for the best. What will really grab their attention is to see their names or initials somewhere on that page. After all, the reader gets your agenda in the mail and the first thoughts go something like, "What does this mean to me?" or "What should I do as a result of this of this piece of paper coming?" You answer that first. To save the reader time and have a better meeting, *indicate by a personalized red tick mark who is responsible for which agenda item.*

When people are able to come to a meeting with their part prepared, then everyone saves time. No one will need to equivocate because they did not understand that they had some essential preparation to bring with them. Of course, if you called the meeting you will need to be prepared too— but that's the main point, isn't it?

6. *Minutes that get Action and Prevent Wasted Meetings*

Sometimes a person will spend hours putting together a comprehensive set of minutes. At the next meeting it is obvious that the minutes were never really read. Who is to blame in this case? In some cases the recording secretary has simply overcommunicated and in other cases the recipient has not considered it important enough to dig through the minutes to find out what was expected. It must be admitted that some minutes are simply a record of what went on and there is no follow-up action.

After you have spent two or three hours at a meeting, you want to be sure that your time hasn't been wasted. When a decision is made there is generally someone responsible for taking action on it. Sometimes further information must be gathered and brought to the next meeting and action is assigned to someone. A good chairman will make sure that persons are assigned to actions during the meeting. Your secretary will have an "action by" column alongside the minutes which notifies each person what is expected from them. This has the further advantage that if the chairman forgets to assign someone to a follow-up item then it becomes clear in the minutes. The minutes of problem-solving meetings can often be quite brief because the main point is to notify people of the part they are to play in further solving of the problem. The minutes might read like this:

MINUTES AND ACTION MEMO

Item	Action by
Delivery of major equipment will be delayed 60 days. To investigate means to compensate for this time loss	J.K.W.
The U.K. has devalued the pound by another 10%. Effects on our exports to be investigated by	Janice K.

So you see from the above that the Retrieval Principle can be applied to agendas and minutes of meetings. The idea is that the reader should be able to scan and very quickly pick out the item which is relevant to them personally. They should be user-oriented.

HOW TO GET THE PAYOFF

The Retrieval Principle is based upon the way the human mind works with all its wonders and its limitations. The principle can be used with those activities that depend upon calling up or transferring significant amounts of important information. This is where the payoff will be. Apply the Retrieval Principle to a few of the activities in the section following on the Guide to Time Mastery and then you will recognize opportunities for applying it to other activities as they arise.

TWO QUESTIONS YOU SHOULD ASK YOURSELF WHEN YOU HAVE IDENTIFIED SUCH AN ACTIVITY

1. "Are there clues which can aid me or the receiver in recalling the information which is to be transferred?"

2. "Can the information be rearranged to better suit the user so that it will save time and be more effective?"

GUIDE TO TIME MASTERY

THE RETRIEVAL PRINCIPLE

Where the performance, P, of an activity depends primarily on the use of stored information, the time, T, will be least when the information was first stored with user-oriented clues.

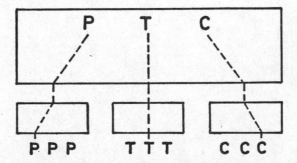

Main Points
1. Because the human mind can store vast amounts of information but can only deliver it slowly, clues are necessary for speedy retrieval.

2. Knowledge and information is transferred effectively when a user-oriented arrangement is employed.

3. You accomplish more when you apply the Retrieval Principle to activities which depend on information gathering and on its transfer to other persons.

What You Should Do

1. Go through the activity list suggested in chapter 1 and enlarge it with your own specific activities. Identify those requiring the gathering or transfer of large amounts of knowledge and information.

2. Can any of these be improved by adding organized clues to the information and knowledge being stored?

3. Can a user-oriented arrangement of the information be made which will enable the user to retrieve and employ it more effectively?

4. Try instructing someone in a complex delegation by first organizing it into modules which can be learned independently.

10

Tips and Techniques For Handling "Priorities Pressure"

KEY IDEA
When all things are urgent, do enough on each to hold the line. Then divide your remaining time among them—using the Division Principle

"BUT BOSS, I JUST CAN'T . . . ."

This could be you or me at some point in our work. See if you can recall a similar situation as you listen in on this imaginary telephone conversation between a purchasing manager and his boss.

"Look John, you know I never say no when you call a meeting but this time I'm asking you to defer it if you can. I need at least one day to catch up on my priorities . . . .What are they? Well, for one, this is the deadline for my budget and you happen to be interested in getting that one done. Then we have a quality control problem on some materials, and I must get into that so we don't lose our warranty by reworking them without permission. It really should be done by that new buyer, Hank, but you know how green he is. Sometime today I have to call a meeting with production and marketing to get a long-term commitment to place an order which will give us a 25% discount if we place it today. That's worth at least $100,000 in savings to the company . . . . What else? Well, one of my key technical advisors has an offer from a competitor, and if I don't get him a raise today he is going to quit. This will involve you and the personnel office because it's going to mean a revision of the salary scales. You know what a hassle that will be. I'll be damn lucky if I can get all these priority items done today. You'll do us both a big favour if you'll get this meeting scheduled for tomorrow instead of today . . . . Yes, I will make myself available for any time you choose tomorrow . . . ."

The purchasing manager put down the phone. He was already in a cold sweat. "Damn it, here it is only 10 o'clock and I'm already swamped with urgent things to do. I feel like that guy in the magician's sword box—one wrong move and I'm finished."

It sometimes happens that you have more priorities than you can handle. Nothing can be delayed. Everything needs some attention. What to do then is explained below.

WHAT YOU WILL GAIN FROM READING THIS CHAPTER

There are times when you are absolutely overloaded with important things to do. When everything is important and there isn't enough time to do them all, then you must be systematic in your approach. This chapter will show how to do it by using the Division Principle.

BENEFITS FROM USING THE DIVISION PRINCIPLE

- You will not feel overwhelmed when you have too many high priorities.
- You will know when to do part of each or do one at a time until completed.
- You will know how to cope with "priorities pressures".

Deciding on what is important in the first place is so important that you should first of all make sure that your priorities are related to purpose as outlined in chapter 3, entitled "How to Decide What is Important". A following chapter on "The Threshold Effect" will also help you when you have too many priorities. The basic approach to the problem of what to do when you have too many priorities is the subject of this chapter.

You will learn about the Division Principle, which is explained by some simple reasoning about betting at the race track. Then I will tell you of how I used the Division Principle myself. This will be followed by six specific techniques for handling "priorities pressures" like bookkeeping; taking over another's mess; crisis on crisis; a late project; priority meetings; and a sick crew. You will also be shown how to apply this principle to your own work and to that of your subordinates.

THE DIVISION PRINCIPLE

Suppose you go to the race track with a fixed amount of dough with which to play the horses. Suppose further that you have no idea of which horse will win. What then is the best strategy?

You might take your lucky rabbit's foot with you or use some strategy of selection by names, but if you have no idea of the track record or capabilities of any of the horses, then you can lose your whole bundle on the first one and that would cause you high regret. There are ways to hedge your bets and win at the track if you know the game, but we will just suppose you are a dum-dum when it comes to horse races (as indeed I am) and you are just there to get the most fun for your money. You know you will have some regret but you wish to minimize the regret and get the most fun you can with your limited bundle.

You could randomly bet part of your bundle on horses by drawing names out of a hat. If you are careful not to bet

too much at a time then you could play for quite a while because you will have some wins and some losses, with the
house cutting in on your average return. However, you
could get exactly the same results by betting an equal
amount on all the horses. You will always win and you will
always lose a little. If you have no idea which horse has the
highest priority, then the equal bet strategy will enable you
to stay in the game for the longest time.

This example of race track betting is just my way of
explaining to you a statistical decision theorem that says, in
effect, that if you have no information on the relative payoff,
then you should give each course of action the same proba-
bility of success—which is the same as betting the same
amount on all the horses, subject to the minimum bet which
is permitted. This is known as the course of action with
minimum regret.

Such a situation can and does arise frequently in management and in business situations. Tasks A, B, C and D can
be equally important in a very short period of time. That is,
there is a high utility for each and they are all urgent. What
is your best strategy? You can bet your time at random. This
will be difficult because you cannot help but be biased toward or against some task. The strategy you can control is to
give an equal amount to each task. So, in a practical sense, if
you have eight hours to do four tasks, you put two hours on
each one—subject to the minimum bet of time which will
now be discussed.

There is a condition on applying equal time to each
task. There is a minimum amount of work that must be done
on any of these before there is any utility for your time.
Otherwise the time will be wasted. So the best strategy in
using the Division Principle is: give the minimum amount
required on each task to bring it above its threshold level;
then divide the remainder of the time among the tasks. It is
clearly better to bring each one above the threshold value
than to do each to completion—like the doctor at the
battlefront who has too many wounded to tend to, he

minimizes losses by doing the minimum necessary to take a wounded soldier out of the danger zone, thereby changing him to a lower priority.

Another way of looking at this principle is that if you do a priority task to the minimum level first, it will be taken out of the high priority category and extra effort can be put on it at a later time. We are now ready to state the Division Principle:

THE DIVISION PRINCIPLE

If a set of tasks are of equal utility and are all of high priority, do each to the threshold value and then divide the remainder of the available time among them.

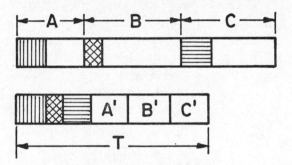

A CASE HISTORY IN WHICH THE DIVISION PRINCIPLE PAID OFF

When I was a manager of applications engineering for a manufacturer of television tubes, there were days when we had to scramble like twelve hungry pups nursing on an eight-nippled mother. The phone rang off the wall. People shouted, harangued and pleaded. I would just get working to solve one problem when the switchboard would have me paged for another. The T.V. manufacturing business was booming and there was a heavy demand for tubes. However, many of these tubes did not work at all well in their T.V. applications because they were primarily designed for radios. The purchasing agent of one of our large customers would call up and say, "Syd, we have another problem out in the factory. I'm going to put one of our engineers on the line to tell you what it's about." We would get into the problem and I would be thinking, "How can I get this one off my back so that I can work on some of the others?"

Company policy was never to admit that anything was wrong, and to try and convince the customer to use the goods anyway. Sometimes it would work but as often as not the customer would come back and say, "Don't try and talk us out of this one. It's costing us $500 an hour to hold up the production line and we have a problem. So do something about it or we're going to start buying somewhere else."

Sometimes we would get three new problems in one day and still have two left over from the day before. There was no question of handling one at a time, because it took weeks to solve the technical problems involved. Nor could we drop any except at our peril. Something had to be done and had to be done fast. My strategy was something like this: What is the minimum I must do to lower the priority of this problem so that we can have a proper look at it in the lab? The tactics within the strategy were (a) replace the tubes with some from another production run if the problem hadn't occurred before, or (b) substitute a tube of another type which is more suitable for the application, or (c) go directly to a solution that worked before in a similar case, if it existed, or (d) convince the customer to take it easy in the case where they were judging the tubes too hard, or (e) check out the problem at once if we had the customer's television set in our lab.

Having done the minimum amount on each problem in order to change its priority, we then took the time remaining to us and shared it among the problems. I would hand a problem to an assistant and say, "See what you can do in two hours or less and then go on to this other problem." In this way we whittled away at the ultimate solution to many problems. At the same time we gave the customers stop-gap measures to reduce their losses of $500 per hour in wages for people who had to wait for the production line to get going again. When the pressure was off we did our more careful investigations, wrote up our reports, and specified changes in our products.

The payoff from our use of the Division Principle was through the service that we provided our customers. They had tangible evidence, each of them, that we were working on their problem and making progress. They put in a good word for us with our employers. We got tangible rewards in the way of substantial pay increases and money for buying the equipment that we wanted. If I had taken the approach of selecting one problem and working it through to its completion before going on with another, then the unattended customers would have crucified me. Instead, I got a reputation in the industry for being an outstanding problem solver.

SIX WAYS YOU CAN USE THE DIVISION PRINCIPLE DURING "PRIORITIES PRESSURE"

1. *What to Do when the Bookkeeping Gets Behind*

The president of a small refrigeration service company found that he was behind in most of the accounting. The invoicing was running late and affecting his cash flow; the monthly close-offs were about three months late in coming to his attention; the project records were horribly behind; and the accounts aging schedule had not been made up for two months. He called in his bookkeeper and asked her what was going on. She told him that the company had been growing very rapidly and the work was getting out of hand. She admitted to being a bit behind on the invoicing and promised to do it just as soon as she finished the next monthly statement. She agreed that the project records were not very current but countered by saying that there was a lot of work in doing the payroll every week. She told him that there was more work than she could possibly do by herself and thought that she should really have an assistant.

The president replied that an assistant was out of the

question because he expected the regular seasonal slump soon. The work would go down to even less than one person's work. What they needed was some way for her to keep up with the work while in the busy season. She would have time left over for other things during the slack season.

The bookkeeper stated that the payroll always had priority, but that invoicing, monthly statements, aging accounts, project records and other things, were all so far behind that they were all urgent. She thought that only he could tell her what she should do besides the payroll.

The president said that he did not have time to direct her to one statement or another. Besides, in order to run his business properly, he needed all of the statements. He needed to have the monthly statement to know whether or not his expenses were out of line, and he needed to have a cash flow statement to know whether he would need to borrow from the bank or not. As far as invoicing went, they could not afford to be late in invoicing a large account or else they would have to borrow more money from the bank.

Finally, he told her to *do a useful amount on each of the jobs and then go on to the next.* For example, on the monthly statement during this rush season, he needed to have a statement only accurate enough to indicate whether or not they were making enough profit. On invoicing, it was the big accounts that they wanted to collect, and he did not mind if she was a bit late on the small ones. In the busy season they only had to be sure that the big ones were done.

The bookkeeper got the idea. Instead of doing each one as accurately as an accountant would do it, she could do something less than perfect during the rush season and the president would accept it. It was better to have approximate figures than none at all. She could note which reports were approximate because of the seasonal rush.

The president also told her that she could skip some of the profit and loss statements during this rush period, because he knew that the business was doing well. The same went for the cash flow forecast. The bookkeeper was then told to divide up the balance of the time equally among the tasks that were getting behind, and to do the best she could once she had passed the minimum acceptable level. Her problem with accounting stemmed from the fact that it is usually worked out to the nearest penny. Accountants pride themselves on the accuracy of their work. The utility of the work done, however, was in the whole set of reports. Any single report, however accurate, was not much use without the others. This was a case of moving forward on all fronts at the best possible pace. The advantage of using the Division Principle was that the business was able to measure itself and move ahead without lacking some essential reports from the bookkeeper.

2. The New Job Is in a Mess but You Can Clean It Up

A marketing executive was hired to replace an incompetent person who really left things in a mess. The morale of the salesmen was low. The advertising was bad. Sales were going down and their market share was declining. The office facilities were inadequate. The shipping and invoicing procedures were antiquated. In all, things were in such a mess that the new marketing manager found it hard to decide what was the highest priority. If sales were down, it might be because of the morale of the salesmen; or the quantity of the advertising; or because the product had quality problems. All of these things were important, and the new marketing manager had to get in there and make a showing.

The marketing manager had consultations with all of his regional sales supervisors and with the key persons in the company. He made a list of all of his problems. He applied the Purpose Principle and gave them priority ratings. At the top of his list were three things which were all interrelated and all of high priority and all requiring his personal attention. However, he realized that if he really went into the advertising matter thoroughly, it would be several months before he could make a decision to change the agency, if indeed this was the solution. If he buried himself in the morale aspects, then the advertising and quality problems might not get enough attention. Since most of the things had to be done during business hours, working overtime would not help much. Therefore, he had to divide up his 40-hour week and work on all of these high priority things, moving ahead on all fronts until the situation was better. To further complicate matters, the president was continually sending down requests for special reports, and the financial executive wanted more accurate sales forecasts. Some of this work could be delegated, yes, but as he was new he was not sure who he could depend on.

What he did was this: To the three major problems he devoted two hours of each day, making six hours in all. This left two or three hours for other matters which were unavoidable. In a few months he had chipped away at the major problems until they had stabilized. Morale wasn't getting any worse because he had transferred an obnoxious sales manager to another job. The quality problem was still being worked on but some temporary fixes had been applied to the product. The advertising problem was still in front of him but he had contracted out some additional advertising with another agency on a trial basis. Of course, these three problems did not move above the threshold level at once. One was ready in a week, another took three weeks, and another took five.

When you take over a new job from someone else, you often find it in a mess. Perhaps it didn't seem to be a mess to the former person, but if often seems like a mess to the new one. The new person can see problems the other person had lived with too long to see. If you cannot put one priority much ahead of another priority, then you should give equal time to each until they start coming above the threshold value. When one problem is stabilized you can put more time on another until it is stabilized. *Then the final application of the Division Principle is to divide your time equally among work tasks which appear to have the same high priority. The payoff in using this approach will be that before very long in a new job you will give convincing proof that something is being done about the problems.* In due course you will solve all of the problems in a methodical and systematic way and your reputation as a good manager will be enhanced.

3. Crisis on Crisis: Cool the Hot Rocks

There is hardly any managerial job which does not have a few crises. Occasionally, one crisis will follow after another, after another, after another, until you feel like a cornered fox with the hounds coming in on all directions. The case of the manufacturing executive of a pulp and paper company is typical. A production problem is normal and this is the regular crisis that a manufacturing executive can handle. But if you add to that a major customer being lost; the government requiring a briefing on your new anti-pollution devices; the legal hassle with your competitors; environmental complaints from the local council; your best manager resigning; the president wanting complete reports on the actions you are taking;—then you are going to cope or look like a dope. You don't have time to sit down and work out priorities. Your priorities are just as clear as if they had just been chiseled in stone and offered to you on a tombstone.

Too often we see people in responsible positions reacting to crises in a panic. They flit from one crisis to another without accomplishing anything, and spend more time trying to cover themselves than getting the problems looked after.

If this crisis-on-crisis situation should happen to you, just get a hold of yourself and cool it. Start moving crises into non-crises by doing the minimum amount, enough to lower the priority. This at least will be a most efficient use of your time and whatever time is left over can then be allocated equally among the important things. In this way you will be working on permanent solutions to the crises while stabilizing the situation. You will be able to get back to your golf with a steady hand and not be nervous about those disasters behind you at the office.

4. Getting a Project Back on the Track

The personnel manager of a midwestern machinery firm had really bungled their move to new quarters. The new building was going to be finished late; the furniture was going to be late; the relocation of families and employees had just begun; and the new equipment was going to be delivered months ahead of when there would be a place to store it. The engineering manager suggested that they put one of their project engineers on the job.

Fortunately for this organization, the project engineer was familiar with the Critical Path Method. He listed all of the activities necessary for the move and then drew out what he called a logic diagram for them. This showed which activities needed to precede which. He estimated the times and costs for all of them. There were a lot of things to be managed, but by using the Critical Path Method the project engineer was able to identify those activities which, if delayed, would hold up the move. He was also able to iden-. tify those which had some slack for completion and did not require his immediate attention. With the limited time at his disposal, he divided his time among the critical activities and got the project on the track again.

In the above example, I have introduced you to a more sophisticated technique of tracking the key activities of a top priority situation. The CPM/PERT techniques used in project management are useful in identifying that sequence of activities which are critical to the completion of a project on time. By having management effort concentrated on these activities, it is not unusual to have everything completed on schedule, particularly one-of-a-kind projects, such as moving into new facilities.

5. How to Cope with too many Top Priority Meetings

An engineering manager joined an aerospace company at the peak of their activity to put a man on the moon. They had hired him away from a competitor because of a special expertise which they themselves had lost through the untimely death of one of their experts. Since the moon shot was definitely scheduled and had to take place on a certain day on a certain month in order to get through the so-called "space window," there was a big rush on using this man's talents for getting the job done. Before he knew it he was scheduled for six meetings a day at which he was either required to comment or just listen in. They were top priority meetings because they were commanded by management, and the company was in a bit of a box at the time.

One late afternoon, when most people had gone for supper, the engineering manager was catching up on his office work and he came across a message from the executive to whom he reported. This was a notification that they would make a three-day trip to Washington to advise the government on some proposed changes in their contract. In addition to that he found other messages and notes requiring him to be at five additional meetings in addition to the six per day that were already scheduled for him. This fantastic load of meetings would not normally occur, but it was just one of those unbelievable situations that can occur in the aerospace industry.

Our manager sat back and considered the situation. The meetings were important and so was the trip to Washington. He liked his job, but he didn't believe it was worth dying for. At this pace he would be worn to a frazzle in a month. It seemed to him that they were trying to do too much in too short a time. What other people considered to be top priority frequently turned out to be something that could easily have waited another month. He had to become tough in order to survive and so this is what he did: He analyzed his regular six meetings and found that his useful input to each varied from ten minutes to one hour. Then he revised his schedule accordingly and drafted letters to each of the meeting chairmen indicating that for the next three weeks he would be tied up in many meetings and trips and asked if they would please schedule his portion of the meeting very tightly. He would be on telephone standby during the meeting. It was imperative that he do some of the deskwork which arose out of the meetings. As for the trip to Washington, he later found that the minimum acceptable level was one meeting there, which only required him to be away for one day plus the travel time. He applied the Addition Principle by doing important work while he was travelling to and from Washington. Whatever time was left to him he divided more or less equally among the top priority tasks that he had been given in connection with the various meetings. This was his application of the Division Principle.

6. *Managing the Work when the Crew is off Sick*

We all get sick sometimes. We can be away from work for one or two days and somehow the managing work still gets done. However, when the specialists are away, the work just piles up. The manager must do something about it. If he understands the work, he can do some of it himself. He may contract it out or he may delegate it to other persons. When a person is away sick for two or three weeks, it frequently adds to the load on the manager.

Imagine, if you will, the situation that Jed found himself in just after the yuletide celebrations. Two of his crew were already away on tropical vacations. Their work had been spread among the rest but for some reason sickness and influenza had knocked out three others. To make matters worse, his girl Friday slipped on the ice and had her kneecap removed. She was now recuperating in the hospital. That put six people out of commission and with an original crew of only ten, it looked like Jed had new priorities. *First he set out to stabilize the situation and move some of the problems to a lower priority.* He got a temporary girl to do his office work and, although she couldn't be an executive assistant, she was a stop-gap insofar as correspondence and telephone answering were concerned. Then he went to work on the work that was piling up for the sick persons and the ones on vacation. *He sorted it into piles of crucial, important, and postponable.* He did the crucial stuff himself. He asked his remaining crew to do the same thing with their work and to take on some of the important items of the sick and missing persons. In this way he kept the office moving along for the next two weeks until his two refreshed team members got back from vacation and started the ball rolling again. Instead of each person going back to his own work, *as long as they were short-handed each person took what were considered crucial and divided his time among them.* They set aside the postponable work until a full crew was at hand to catch up on it.

It would have been easy for Jed to make excuses for the operation of his office, since more than half of his crew was sick or away. Everybody has sicknesses to contend with at one time or another so his superiors would be understanding—up to a point, that is. Jed had the right idea. Even with half the crew he managed to keep the ship afloat and moving along in the right direction. This was a good application of the Division Principle.

OBTAINING THE BENEFITS OF THE DIVISION PRINCIPLE

The time to apply the Division Principle is when you have too many high priority items for the time available. You handle this not by doing one at a time, but by doing the minimum amount on each high priority job, so that the rest of it is postponable. This gains you relief from priority pressures and enables you to divide your remaining time among the remaining important work.

It is equally important to know when *not* to use the Division Principle. When one of the tasks is definitely a higher priority than the others, then you do it. If one has a high utility and can be done in a very short time then you do that in preference to others—but when the time comes that you have more priorities than you can handle, you will apply the Division Principle.

When you learn how to apply the Division Principle in the priority pressures situation, you will not feel overwhelmed by the combined magnitude of the tasks. You will know that you can do part of each with your prime time and divide the rest of your time among the remainder. You will then be coping with the priority pressures.

You know full well that practice makes perfect. If you have found that some of the examples and techniques above apply to your job, then go to it. If you want this principle to be a life-long friend, then go through the following exercises which will guide you to the mastery of time.

GUIDE TO THE MASTERY OF TIME

THE DIVISION PRINCIPLE

If a set of tasks are of equal utility and are all of high priority, do each to the threshold value and then divide the remainder of the available time among them.

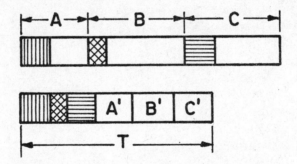

Main Points

1. Priorities are established by a combination of serving your purposes and their urgency.

2. There are situations where the time required for completing all the high priority tasks before you is simply more than you have available.

3. In such a situation it is not wise to do one at a time and not do anything on one of the important priorities.

4. A little effort on each is better than full effort on some, provided that the minimum amount on each task is done in order to lower its current priority.

Applying the Division Principle

In order to use this principle you must become aware of your present behaviour in a crisis situation, and then program yourself to behave differently when the situation arises again.

1. When you were last faced with a load of high priority items, which of the following did you do?
   (a) panic,
   (b) do some and neglect the others,
   (c) methodically do one at a time until they were all done,
   (d) put in an enormous amount of extra hours until all were done,
   (e) do the minimum amount required for each and do what you could on the remainder,
   (f) other.

2. Can you think of some time when your whole organization was in a state of crisis upon crisis? Who panicked? Who went straight on as if there was no crisis? Think of someone who might have been using the Division Principle. What were **you** doing in that situation?

3. Is there a time of the year when you are almost sure to have too many high priority jobs to do?

4. Make a mental memo to yourself for when you next have too many high priority items. You will ask yourself, "Should I do a minimum on each and then divide my time among them?".

5. Do you know of a subordinate who you could help in handling a crisis-on-crisis situation? Instructing someone else will clarify your own understanding of the principle. It will be helpful to you to have your subordinates trained in the Division Principle, because the time will come when the heat will be on you, and you will want to delegate a group of high priority items to someone who can handle them effectively. So prepare your subordinates.

11

What to Do When You Can't Do Everything

KEY IDEA
How to separate the vital few from the trivial many—using the Pareto Principle.

TOO MANY CALLS TO MAKE

A sales manager of an appliance manufacturing company was concerned about the performance of one of his salesmen. Although the salesman worked like a beaver his sales were continuously below the quota based upon the performance of other salesmen. The manager decided to take a day with the man in the field and find out what he was doing.

What the sales manager noticed was that the salesman called on almost every appliance store in town, whether they were an authorized appliance dealer of his company or not. His personality was good, his sales techniques adequate and by and large the dealers were glad to see him. When questioned about this practice, the salesman replied that every appliance store was a potential customer and that he should distribute his time between well established dealers and new potentials. The salesman, however, regretted that there were some towns that he was unable to do properly. Though he worked from dawn to dusk he could not find time to call on all of the dealers.

After an exhausting day on the road, the sales manager and the salesman were relaxing over the evening libation when the sales manager said something like: "Have you ever heard of the Pareto Principle? No? Well, I think it applies in your case. Probably one-fifth of your calls account for 75% of the sales you will make. When you can't call on every prospect then you should concentrate on the vital few who buy the most. That's the principle. I think we should apply it to your selling effort."

WHAT YOU WILL LEARN FROM THIS CHAPTER

There will be times in your career when you will be subject to prolonged periods of overload. You simply can't get everything done and something is going to be set aside or deferred. This is a hard choice to make because you are expected to do all the things for which you are responsible, and normally you are staffed adequately to do so. If you are in a chronic overload condition, then there may be something wrong with you or the number of staff that you have. But assuming that you can handle the work on the average workload, what is the best thing to do when you are overloaded?

In the following pages you will learn about the Pareto Principle—separating the vital few from the trivial many. A few of your activities contribute much to the accomplishment of your purposes, but there are many others that contribute only a little. You will accomplish most with your time if you concentrate on the vital few during a period of prolonged overload. You will find that the Pareto Principle is another way to extend your use of the Purpose Principle, learned in chapter 3, and budgeting your time, learned in chapter 4. These principles applied when it was possible to do all of the things you were expected to do. So now we will extend these into the situation where you simply can't do everything. The Pareto Principle will guide you when you haven't time to systematically set priorities of tasks and plan a schedule of maximum utility such as described in chapters 3 and 4.

BENEFITS OF USING THE PARETO PRINCIPLE

1. You will get the highest utility for the time that is available.
2. You will tend to feel more comfortable about setting some things aside in order to do the vital few.
3. You will help your subordinates identify the vital few from the trivial many when they are in an overload situation.

In this chapter, the Pareto Principle will be explained and then you will read a case history telling how John B. and I put it to good use. Then there will be three specific techniques to use in management: daily priorities; returning telephone calls; and being selective about going to meetings.

At the end of the chapter there will be guidelines to the mastery of time by using the Pareto Principle for identifying the vital people and activities in your own work.

THE PARETO PRINCIPLE

It should be obvious that some of the work you do is vital and other activities are trivial—some have high importance and others have low importance with respect to your purposes. Now what is often obvious can be studied and put into mathematical law. A famous Swiss economist named Vilfredo Pareto did this in the 19th century. He studied the distribution of incomes and found that not only were some persons immensely rich, but that most of the wealth was concentrated in the hands of a few. This was true in a number of countries where he did his investigations. He was able to give this finding a mathematical formulation. A few people controlled most of the wealth in these countries, and large humbers of people had very little. This is self evident in large parts of the world but I am not so sure it applies in modern free enterprise countries such as the United States. Nevertheless, I am told by others that within any industry, say steel or oil, the economic power is concentrated in the hands of a few corporations. The vital industries can be found, and the vital corporations within any industry can be identified. So, if Pareto were alive today, he would be able to find data which would support his principle.

On a more practical scale, you can find many examples of the vital few and the trivial many in everyday business. For instance, if customers are listed in order of their sales volume you will probably find that about 20% of the customers account for 80% of the sales volume. Likewise, if you have a large product line you will probably find that 20% of the products result in 80% of the profit. The other 80% of products are only contributing about 20%. This is the 80/20 rule that is also an outgrowth of Pareto's thought.

Take the situation of the typical manager or executive. He will have many activities and tasks for which he is responsible. Some of these contribute much to the company's purposes and others contribute marginal amounts. This concept is difficult for us to see individually in ourselves, but it generally is very apparent if we look at subordinates. When they evaluate themselves, then everything they do is important. When we evaluate them, it's different. Some things are vital and others are trivial. This is why "Management by Objectives" has been so effective in some organizations. The importance of tasks and activities is determined by their contribution to objectives. Objectives are simply statements of purposes, and this gets us back to an earlier chapter which discussed the Purpose Principle. When you have purposes, the things you do towards these purposes cannot contribute equally. It is certainly true in managerial work or any business endeavour. You should not be confused with mass production where each unit done contributes equally to the results. A manager or professional organizes his own time and also does creative work. He or she also goes through periods of high activity where not everything gets done. Like the doctor with an overload of patients, you give your best time to the vitally important problems, and give a short shift to the trivia. The Pareto Principle can be stated as follows:

THE PARETO PRINCIPLE

A small portion of your activities are vital and these contribute the most towards your purposes. A large portion of your activities are trivial in their contribution towards your purposes.

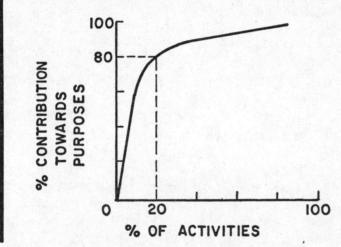

CASE HISTORY: CAN WE REALLY PLEASE EVERYBODY?

John B. reported to me as a manager of components testing. He was responsible for approving the sources of the purchased components we used in our products. He also investigated many component problems and participated with the vendors in the develpment of better components. John was well suited for this job because of his 'nice guy' attitude. He saw himself as the manager of a service organization and he wanted to be able to please everyone. He was liked for his responsive and sympathetic understanding of people's problems. However, his efforts to please everybody were his downfall during the prolonged period of work overload that occurred at least once a year. His staff was adequate for the average work, but when new products were being pushed into production in the fall, there usually was a backlog of work.

Complaints about the operation of the components testing unit came to me through high-level channels. The purchasing department complained that they had many opportunities for second, third and fourth sources which the components testing unit failed to approve in time for use in production. The buyers felt that they were not able to effectively save the company money because of the long delay in getting the approval through. The first complaint was coupled with a statement that they liked John himself and thought maybe he was simply more responsive to work pressures from engineering than he was to the purchasing department.

When I talked to John about the problem, I found that he had considerable personal stress because of the tug-of-war between his personal loyalties to buyers and to members of the engineering department; limitations of the capacity of his equipment; the urgency of some of the approvals because of the need to buy for production. He had a backlog of three months work but if someone got on the phone and urged him to move up the priority of their request he did his best to comply.

The first thing I pointed out was that in this period of overload we simply couldn't do everything that was asked of us. His problem was not priorities, but what not to do at all. We needed to have a rationale for not doing certain things because others clearly had a higher priority. After some discussion we came up with a priority list for his activities. It was as follows:

1. Investigate component problems which are holding up production.

2. Process first source approvals of components according to their urgency.

3. Process second source approvals on the basis of the dollars saved in total, obtained by multiplying the unit cost savings times the volume that would be purchased.

4. Process third and fourth source approvals based upon the total dollars saved.

5. Development of more reliable components (last because there would be time later in the year to place a higher priority on this activity).

Our priorities were then explained to the purchasing manager. He saw at a glance that engineering problems got the highest priority as he suspected, but we were able to assure him that this kept production running smoothly and that other engineering work was set aside. As to the approval of the second and third sources, he was glad to see that it was being done on a profitability basis, and agreed that those things which would not get done would be those with the low profit return. We also agreed that there would be exceptions, but we asked that the buyers not try and change the priorities through their personal influence on John. By using these guidelines the vital things would get done and the trivia would be set aside. We were using the Pareto Principle—that is what this chapter is about.

THREE WAYS YOU CAN USE THE PARETO PRINCIPLE

1. Try a Stack of Cards

Try doing what Robbie M. of Ottawa did. He had a lot of things to do, not only studies requested by the organization he served; not only urgent telephone calls; not only meetings; but many things he initiated himself. He did a lot and wanted to do more. He came to one of my time management seminars and was taken by the idea of using cards to sort out his priorities. He went one step further though and, without knowing it, was applying the Pareto Principle. When he could not do everything, he made sure that he did the vital things with the time he had. Here is the technique.

THE PARETO STACK OF CARDS

1. List each activity or task that is ahead of you on a 3×5 card.
2. Sort them into a priority ranking with respect to your purposes.
3. Put the pile on your desk, with the highest priority on top.
4. Do the card at the top of the pile first. (Then file it or discard it.)
5. When a new thing to do arises, make out a card and put it into the pile in its appropriate priority relative to the others.
6. Re-sort the stack of cards daily, because priorities change with urgency.

Robbie had a neat way of finishing off a task. Instead of filing the card away as a record of what he had done, he got great pleasure from throwing it forcibly into the trash can. In this way he got a sense of accomplishment, which rewarded him for doing the task. Another point that Robbie mentioned was that he no longer procrastinated. The most important thing for him to do was facing him on the top of that card pile.

I can add another point. At the end of a day when you have more to do than you can possibly do, there will be some cards left over. You can tell yourself that you have nevertheless got the biggest payoff for your time by concentrating on the vital few and setting aside the trivial many.

2. Return the Vital Telephone Calls

When you get back to your office after several days absence, you may have a long list of telephone calls to return. If your secretary has been working on your behalf (and by your instructions) she has solicited something brief from each caller about the nature of the call. She has probably clipped a few of the messages together with a tag marked "urgent."

With or without your secretary's preparation, you could take a look at the priorities on these telephone calls. You should assume that some of them will not get done immediately. You return a call and the other person isn't there. You're not sure if the call was vital or not so you may be inclined to place the call again. Some callers will be using their telephones and you can't even leave a message, so again more time is lost.

There are also people that you want to call and they should be added to your slips. Sort them into piles of vital, questionable, and trivial, and then mark them three star, two star and one star. **Concentrate on the three star vital calls** that must be returned or made. You are doing this because you are aware that all the telephone calls that are to be returned are not of equal importance. On the scale of courtesy they may be of equal importance but on a scale of contribution to your job purposes they will not be. Right? Now you really understand Pareto's thoughts about vital few, and now you can apply it to many things that you do.

3. Be Selective about Going to Meetings

Many managers and executives report to me that their whole work day is scheduled with meetings. They must come in early and stay late in order to get any work done. They are invited to many meetings and they don't like to turn anyone down or miss out on anything that's going on. Consequently *they find themselves outer-directed.* Other people are taking their time from them whereas they should be planning their own time. Time is the gift of life. It belongs to you exclusively. You can *give* it, or other people can *take* it. It is up to you to manage your personal resource of time.

There is another way of looking at time spent on meetings. Your working day is bought and paid for by your employer and therefore it is company time. Are you using it effectively by attending all of the meetings that you are invited to? Should you be selective? Consider the situation in which you are involved in more meetings than you can afford to attend and still get your other work done. Then you must be selective. There are some meetings which are vital to your work and to your career. There are others which are trivial. Probably after you have attended some others you will feel that they were utter nonsense.

Think of it this way. A meeting is either a three star vital, a two star question, or a one star trivia. **You will go yourself to the three star meetings** because you are wearing the most shoulder pips. **When you are busy you will send subordinates to the two star ones.** As for the lowly one star meetings, you will avoid them and get a copy of the minutes.

Of course, it must be admitted that you may not be the most popular guy if you decline meetings called by others. Is getting ahead dependent on winning a popularity contest or is it dependent on getting results with the time that has been bought and paid for? You, of course, must decide that. It's your own time, remember. In the long run other people can *take* it from you but only you can *give* it. Try rebuilding your schedule as shown in Figure11-1.

OBTAINING THE BENEFITS OF USING THE PARETO PRINCIPLE

There will be times you can't do everything and something must give. They can occur in your business life, your private life, or a combination of both. Those overload times can result from requests to do something within your responsibility or they can be largely self-initiated. If self-initiated, you will have a big list of things to do and it only remains for you to handle it sensibly. Don't drive yourself trying to get everything done when some things are trivial. The Pareto Principle applies to many situations. Remember this rule of thumb—**the vital few and the trivial many**. Or you may think of it mathematically—20% of the tasks I do get 80% of the results.

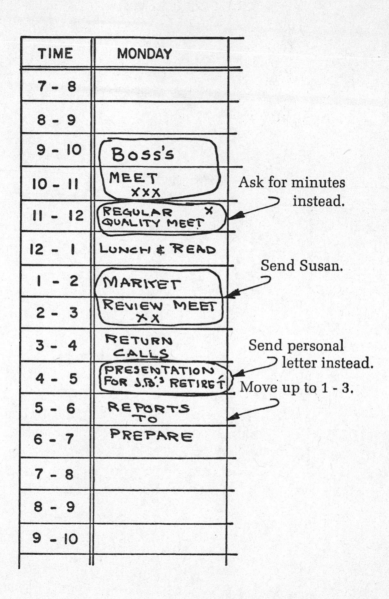

TIME	MONDAY
7 - 8	
8 - 9	
9 - 10	BOSS'S
10 - 11	MEET XXX
11 - 12	REGULAR QUALITY MEET X
12 - 1	LUNCH & READ
1 - 2	MARKET
2 - 3	REVIEW MEET XX
3 - 4	RETURN CALLS
4 - 5	PRESENTATION FOR J.B.'S RETIRE'T
5 - 6	REPORTS TO
6 - 7	PREPARE
7 - 8	
8 - 9	
9 - 10	

Ask for minutes instead.

Send Susan.

Send personal letter instead.

Move up to 1 - 3.

Figure 11-1: Revising Scheduled Meetings
to Gain Back *Your* Time

GUIDE TO THE MASTERY OF TIME

THE PARETO PRINCIPLE
A small portion of your activities are vital and these contribute the most towards your purposes. A large portion of your activities are trivial in their contribution towards your purposes.

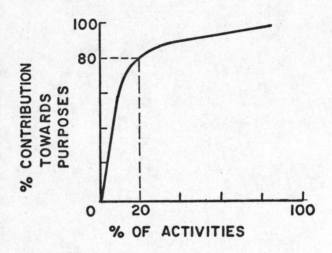

Main Points
1. If a set of tasks are put into order by contribution to your purposes, then about 20% of the tasks will account for 80% of the accomplishment.
2. A simple ordering of your tasks can be three star vital, two star questionable and one star trivial.
3. When you can't do everything, be sure to do what is vital.

Applying the Pareto Principle

1. Try carrying some 3 × 5 cards with you for one week, as outlined in technique number 1. The cards can fit in your shirt pocket, vest, purse, wallet or notebook. You can have them with you wherever

you are. It is important that they be with you so that you can review them frequently and also add other notations. Be sure to mark the three star vital things to do. If the card system works for you, stay with it.

2. If you have the kind of job which enables you to have a schedule of your work as suggested in chapter 4, then mark the vital items with three stars. If you must reschedule your time you will not miss out the vital things.

3. Make a list of all the persons you have frequent contact with, and then pick out the vital few with respect to your job purposes. Are you really oriented to concentrate your contacts on the vital few, or are you involved with the trivial many?

4. Make a list of your subordinates. Which ones are really vital to the organization and which ones are making trivial contributions? Loud noises aren't necessarily vital contributions. This, by the way, is not a personality evaluation. The most human person on your list may end up on the trivial side because he or she may not have some specialized knowledge that the organization needs. This list is yours to use in confidence. If you're ever forced to make a major cutback you will know on which people the survival of the organization depends. You also have a chance to look at your reward system to see whether or not the vital few are being encouraged to stay with the organization.

5. You can apply the Pareto Principle to making a list of customers; a list of vendors; a list of public relations media; and so forth. In other words, make a conscious effort to put the Pareto Principle to other uses right now. With such an analysis of your work you may be able to guide yourself and subordinates to concentrate efforts on the vital few when you can't possibly do all the trivial many.

6. Go to the activity list that you prepared from chapter

1 or some other chapter and mark the vital few with three stars. These should be the things which must be taken care of if you are away from work for any extended period. Use it as a checklist if you are planning an extended trip.

12

Getting
The Most
For the Least

KEY IDEA
You can underdo or overdo a task. Between these extremes, you get the most for your effort—using the Threshold and Saturation Principle.

UNDERDONE AND OVERDONE INTERVIEWS AND MEETINGS

Betty B. was the personnel manager of a large insurance firm in Connecticut. The number of persons with "problems" who were referred to her office for counseling had increased to the point where she scheduled two days every week for interviews with persons having problems. It was really all the time she could afford because of her other commitments. Besides, the work was exhausting because of the emotions involved.

To be fair to everyone, Betty scheduled them at 30 minute intervals which meant she could see 16 people in a week. She was honest, fair, and firm. She kept her appoint-

ments on time, but she was unsatisfied with her results.
People would come in with a light problem such as changing their insurance beneficiary or a special claim on medical
insurance, and these problems were handled with ease.
Other people had a personal problem in their home life and
it seemed to Betty that many times she didn't really get to
the bottom of the problem. This forced her to make decisions based upon incomplete information. Some people
were so silent for the first 25 minutes that she felt the whole
interview was a waste of time.

What was happening to Betty was a failure to recognize
the *threshold effect*. In her interviews there was a minimum
amount of time before she would get anywhere at all and
this would vary from interview to interview. After passing
the threshold she would make rapid progress, but with
some people the threshold was never reached.

It would have been better for Betty to schedule interviews beginning on the hour, with other work to do in intervals between. If an interview lasted only 15 minutes, she
could take up the spare time with other office work. If an interview ran a full hour she could merely defer some of her
other work. If more time was needed she could probably
schedule it again the same day and thereby avoid underdone interviews.

Betty B., like yourself, is often involved in management
meetings which seem to go on and on. Sometimes there is a
poor chairman who continually looks for additional trivia,
or summarizes, or reiterates, long after the points have been
made. Sometimes you get grandstanding between two
people in the meeting who are really making loud noises in
order to impress their colleagues (so they think). After a
while, either the points have been made and the problems
have been solved; or there is not enough information, and
more effort is not producing any results. This is known as
the *saturation effect*. At this point additional time and additional effort will produce very little more accomplishment.

The meeting is being overdone. For the efficient use of your time you need to work between the threshold and saturation effects.

WHAT THIS CHAPTER WILL DO FOR YOU

As seen from the situations above, a task can be underdone or overdone. However, between these extremes, any additional effort is rewarded by additional accomplishment. As is often the case, some tasks seem similar and you arrange to put equal time on them. Although you have control of your time you may not be getting results in proportion to the time. Knowledge of the Threshold and Saturation Principle will enable you to accomplish more in the same time.

BENEFITS TO BE GAINED BY USING THE THRESHOLD AND SATURATION PRINCIPLE

1. You will avoid doing too much or too little on a task.
2. You will work on a task in the efficient region.
3. You will learn to guide your subordinates on the level of accomplishment versus the effort that you expect on each new task.

The principle in this chapter is unique and probably different from anything you have read about before. It is, however, related to the Purpose Principle of chapter 3 because without purpose there is no level of saturation of accomplishment. More work can mean more output, but not necessarily more effectiveness. So that you can learn to use this principle as a unique tool in the management of time, this chapter contains a case history about opening up a new market area, and also a case history about going overboard on quality control. This is followed by eleven specific ways to put the principle to work, such as for writing reports, running a meeting, and using the telephone.

Finally, there are guidelines for applying the Threshold and Saturation Principle to your Mastery of Time.

THE THRESHOLD AND SATURATION PRINCIPLE

Suppose you are writing a report on some research you have done. You will need at least the titles, index, introduction and some key results to get above the threshold level of reporting anything worthwhile. This might be one or two pages. Then additional reporting will amplify the key results and report the minor results. More reporting can elaborate on how the analysis and tests were done. Then you can add appendices with the names and qualifications of the people working on the report; an annotated bibliography; the original experimental results . . .wait, hold your horses! I think we are getting into a saturation effect here. Who is going to read the report? Will you reach the saturation point insofar as their reading is concerned?

Let's look at another example: Weekly meetings with individual subordinates in order to review their work. Some come well prepared and get beyond the threshold and into the action very rapidly. Some will come unprepared or be cagey, so you must dig and dig just to get to the threshold level. Occasionally someone will come overprepared. They will have written reports, documents and hot air that push you quickly into the saturation level.

Here is another example. An engineer, a dentist or technician likes to have good test equipment. They pile it up into a visible display high above their bench. Equipment becomes a status symbol. Bill wants a superexpensive instrument because Joe has got one as good as the state of the art will allow. You can see that the capital equipment per person can get into the saturation area if you are not careful. On the other hand, there is a minimum amount of test equipment for a technical person, which is required in order for them to be effective at all. That is the threshold effect.

You may be familiar with the threshold and saturation effect of sound. Below a certain level you really can't understand anything, and louder than loud has little effect because you are already deaf with the noise. All sensations or feelings are like this. The threshold and saturation effect are basic to the physiological and psychological makeup of a human being.

We are now ready to make a statement about the Principle.

THE THRESHOLD AND SATURATION PRINCIPLE

For any task there is a threshold of effort, below which nothing significant is accomplished. There is also a saturation of accomplishment where additional effort contributes very little. Between the threshold and saturation, the accomplishment is proportional to the effort.

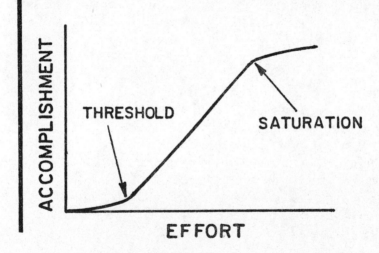

SUCCESSFULLY OPENING UP A NEW MARKET AREA

An electrical appliance manufacturer in New York wanted to increase sales. In ten years since their founding they had developed a comfortable position with sales of about $200,000,000 in the eastern states alone. They had good capital reserves and felt that it was now time to ex-

pand their marketing effort. Further expansion in the eastern states was favored by the president but the marketing
manager was less than enthusiastic about that approach. Instead, he was all enthused about the western states. An untapped market was there for them to pick up. Now the president had a lot of faith in the marketing manager's opinion,
but after all, the president owned the company and it was
his money. To resolve the matter they employed a consultant.

The consultant's report indicated that because the
*company was close to saturation for their market in the
eastern states*, it would require double the effort to get 10%
more sales. Moreover, they would continually have to fight
to maintain a higher penetration of this market because of
counter-efforts by their competition. It would be like driving a Volkswagen beetle up a long grade. You put the pedal
to the floor and the engine noise changes—but the car
doesn't really move much faster.

In the far west there was an untapped market potential
at least half as large as the eastern market they now enjoyed.
Those few western cities which were being developed by a
few select agents showed that the product was acceptable.
However, before this market could be properly penetrated,
there was a minimum investment required to establish
warehouses, to develop service centers, and for high initial
promotion costs. In other words, *not much would happen in
the west until the threshold effort was passed* and this
would take a large proportion of the company's reserve capital. In the meantime, if business took a bad turn, they
would have to borrow money. This was something the president did not want to do. This western situation could be
likened to a very cold engine just starting up. It sputters,
moves along but doesn't really take off until it's warmed up
beyond the threshold point.

The midwest was an area that hadn't been seriously
considered for expansion, but the consultant pointed out to
them that their products had been promoted in the midwest

for several years and were known to the dealers who would sell them. Currently their products were sold by distributors in this area. It would be possible for the company to take over the market developed by these distributors and put their own salesmen on the road. In other words, *this market was ready to go and results would be in proportion to effort.* Like the car that is warmed up and ready, step on the gas and away it goes.

What the appliance manufacturer did was to go into direct selling in the midwestern regions a couple of states at a time. They trained and developed their expanding sales force with a low investment and the sales profit enabled them to expand further into the midwest. They are now at the point where their cash flow is so good and the capital reserves are so healthy that they are ready to enter the far west and put it above the threshold level.

AN OVERBOARD EFFORT ON QUALITY

There was a time during my early experience as a manager of television engineering, that the quality of our products was our uppermost problem. Every day there would be bad news from the production unit about parts not fitting together well or something not looking right. Every week we would get a life test report which would indicate that too many components were failing. We were busy every day and weekends just putting out fires. We would fix up one problem and a new one would rear its demonic head. Sometimes the fix for one problem was the cause of another. We were so busy on these quality problems that we had no time to properly redesign the TV sets or bring out new products.

The paramount cause of our problem seemed to be appointment of a new quality control manager who had orders from the president to put his foot down and not permit any more TV sets of questionable quality to be shipped. Armed with this authority and responsibility, quality control was rigidly enforced. Since many of the problems concerned appearance items and life testing conditions, which were largely subjective, a lot of time was spent on arguments between engineering, quality control, and production. they seldom agreed on whether a "problem" was really a serious one or not.

Let me say that I leaned heavily on better quality myself because the problems had been generated before my time on the job. Before long, however, I noticed that the engineering team was becoming badly demoralized. A few of our good engineers quit and a few others were speaking of leaving. The engineering department had become a whipping boy for all the problems, whereas in fact they were the only people who could correct the problems. They were being beaten over the head with problems on quality. It soon reached the saturation point. Further complaints about quality tended to fall on deaf ears.

Faced with this situation I asked senior management to call off the dogs for awhile to permit us to concentrate on the most serious problems. This meant that some of the subjective "problems" would be passed over for the time being. In this way we were able to get some results for our efforts. Because we were then able to achieve some viable results, morale was once again good. We were no longer "saturated" with complaints. As morale picked up and problems diminished, all things were taken care of in good time.

11 IDEAS FOR SAVING TIME BY USING THE THRESHOLD AND SATURATION PRINCIPLE

1. Delegate a Task that You Cannot Bring Above the Threshold Yourself

If you cannot bring a task up above the threshold level in accomplishment then your effort is wasted. It is better to delay it until you can put more time into it. You may satisfy yourself with some preparatory work just to move the task along. Of course, if you have a task which you can never bring above the threshold level, then you should never do it. Better not done—or done by someone else. This, of course, is **a good reason for delegating. Though you have the expertise to do it well, you may not have the time to bring it up above the threshold value.** Your subordinate may not be able to do it as expertly, but will do a better job than you can do because he will be able to bring it well above the threshold value.

2. How to Decide on Whether or Not to Read a Long Report

You do not need to take time to read the whole thing, but you do need to read enough to understand the summary and conclusion. You save time by looking at these first in order to bring yourself to the threshold value. Then you can decide whether more effort will get more results.

3. Start Out Right to Learn a New Subject

Learning something like a new language, or mathematics, has a threshold value. Repetitive memorizing you can do a nibble at a time, but to learn a new subject you first need some time for concentration and uninterrupted thinking. Better you should schedule sufficient time than to fiddle around and waste time below the threshold level.

4. Get a Good Start on Preparing the Annual Budget

You can do a nibble at a time working on its preparation, getting material sent to you, and filling a file folder. However, to do something as important as this, you must schedule proper time to do it at least to the level of acceptability. You cannot eliminate it but you cannot do it in short passes either.

5. Do Not Underdo or Overdo Performance Interviews

With some "problem" persons you need time to dig into the basic causes of the real problem. A reprimand or a putdown will appear to save you time, but in the long run will be a waste of time if the problem is not resolved. Better you should schedule sufficient time getting to the heart of the problem. Then watch out for the saturation effect. Once you both get talking, you may not want to stop.

6. Decide on Which Articles You Want to Read

You look at the title, scan the abstract and figures and if you think, "This I want to read but I don't have the time to pass the threshold point," mark it for your secretary to get you a copy and read it during your travelling time.

7. Watch Those Inventory Counts

Routine work is so well understood, it is possible to do it near to perfection. For example, it takes no great talent to take a stationery inventory. The talent lies in estimating the number of sheets of paper instead of counting them.

I was once working on a warehouse inventory where all of the nuts, bolts, resistors, condensers and other components were counted individually. Now, it so happened that the organization required exactly enough to finish a production run, with very few left over but absolutely none under. Nevertheless, the general hardware didn't need to be counted to a high degree of precision for the first time around. Only those with low counts needed careful counting. This was a case of overdoing an inventory.

Another case of overdoing an inventory is reconciling cash balances to the nearest penny. An organization will spend $100 in overtime to find 6¢ out of book balance. Smarter organizations are leaving in the minor unbalances and keeping them in a separate ledger because they tend to balance out in the long run.

8. Ways to Avoid Overdoing a Letter

Free-wheeling dictation often results in a verbose letter, whether dictating to a secretary or to a recording machine. There is something about the opportunity to sound-off that makes people say more than they need to. Like talking, over-communicating can make your reader weary. They wonder, "Where is the point?"

WAYS TO GET THE MOST FOR YOUR EFFORT IN WRITING A LETTER

1. If you have dictated it, don't be afraid to chop it heavily.

2. If you tend to be long-winded in your dictation, first make up a ten word outline of the points you want to make.

3. Use space, underlining or script for emphasis. Use subtitles and colored inks, especially if the letter runs more than one page. You want to be sure that your main points pass beyond your reader's threshold of perception. Don't be afraid to use wide spaces for emphasis, such as for separating a paragraph from the others for emphasis.

9. Watch the Time on the Telephone

A simple poll of your acquaintances will tell you whether or not you tend to be long-winded on the telephone. If you are, it's time you do something about it because its *your time* as well as the other person's time.

On the other hand, if you are busy you do not like another long-winded person to take up *your time.* Yet it is difficult to unhook yourself from some people without being unpleasant. Here is an idea for training yourself and your regular callers. Get a cooking timer with a scale of 60 minutes. Set it to ring at a reasonable period after the start of your telephone conversation (whether you are the guilty one or not). When it rings, it will alert you and your caller to the fact that valuable time is passing. You may be going into saturation.

10. Making a Meeting Productive

First, get above the threshold level as quickly as you can by having the updating reports made brief. You should be able to sense when you are able to say, "Are we ready to get down to business now?" Once past the threshold you can obtain maximum results for your efforts.

You will know when the meeting starts to run down. Some people will be flapping their lips just for effect and other people will be leaning away from the talker. At this point, productivity is about zilch and you had better take the gains that you have and go on to something else. Further time at the saturation level will be mostly wasted.

11. *Making an Effective Presentation*

At any meeting, *you need to get your audience above the threshold level*. This is your introduction of background material and refreshers so that people get into the picture. Once there, you can make your points rapidly and emphatically. You are in the productive portion. *Before you reach saturation, reiterate your points and then close it.* If they want to know more, there can be questions.

How do you know when you are reaching saturation? This may not depend only on your presentation. What has gone on before has quite an effect. When the audience is already fatigued, you're better off to make a short presentation and make a few points rather than try to get everything across at a point when nothing is being assimilated. Watch your audience. When people are leaning forward they are interested. When they're leaning forward and holding their chins up with their hands, their heads are heavy and they have lost interest. When they are leaning back away from you, they are thinking of leaving the room. When it's time for lunch they will be taking sideways glances at the clock. When they're snoring, whether standing or sitting, it is already too late. You are past the saturation point.

MAKE THE THRESHOLD AND SATURATION PRINCIPLE WORK FOR YOU

Firstly, you should realize that the utility of something is not the same as the work done on it. A thing can be overdone or underdone. In other words, accomplishment is something not proportional to effort. However, between

saturation and threshold we can roughly equate accomplishment and effort; this is a most efficient region to be
working in.

The Threshold and Saturation Principle is a basic principle of physiology. All sensations have threshold and saturation values. The appreciation of any piece of work is
based on the same principle. So is accomplishment of purpose. There is threshold and there is saturation. The best
appreciation of a piece of work, like appreciation of sensa-
tion, is between the extremes of threshold and saturation.

You should examine every major task that you have
ahead of you and identify threshold and saturation amounts
of effort. Then you should decide what level is the best for
each situation. Follow the Guide below.

GUIDE TO TIME MASTERY

THE THRESHOLD AND SATURATION PRINCIPLE

For any task there is a threshold of effort, below
which nothing significant is accomplished. There is also
a saturation of accomplishment where additional effort
contributes very little. Between the threshold and saturation, accomplishment is proportional to the effort.

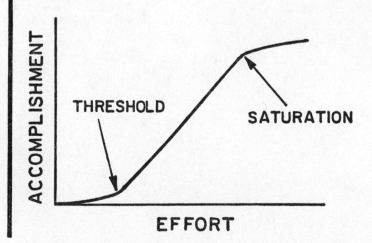

Main Points

1. A task has a threshold level of effort below which your time is wasted.
2. Most tasks have a saturation level of effort beyond which little more is gained for additional time.
3. The best use of your time on a task is between the regions of threshold and saturation.

Action to be Taken for Time Mastery

1. Go to the list of activities and tasks that you developed in chapter 1, or subsequently. Identify any that you believe are usually done into the saturation region. Can you do less of these and switch your time to some better use?

2. Go to the list again and this time identify some activities or tasks which are usually done below the threshold level. Should you arrange to delegate them, should you eliminate them, or should you schedule enough time to get them above the threshold level?

3. When you have a new task to delegate to your subordinate, take time to think through what you would consider the threshold and saturation levels of effort. Indicate to your subordinate what level of result you would like to get before having them commit themselves to undertaking the work. This procedure will save you both time in the long run.

13 Practical Ways to Increase Your Ability To Accomplish More

KEY IDEA
There are specific areas where you can easily increase your ability and thus save time—using the Input-Output Principle.

Fred B. was a top notch technician who reported to me while I was an engineering manager. At one of his annual performance reviews, we discussed his career objectives and he told me this:

He wanted to get ahead but his career opportunities in engineering seemed to be blocked by his lack of a formal degree. He was as good or better in product design than many engineers we had, but although the company gave lip service to merit-based opportunities, it was evident that most of the engineering management positions went to degree engineers. Not only that, but leadership of some of the prestigious technical projects went to graduate engineers, whereas he often felt that he was better qualified to do the job. He was well aware of the legal restraints imposed on the company with regard to people doing engineering work and

231

he was not complaining of any unfair treatment. He merely wanted to point out that he thought the best way for him to get ahead was through non-engineering management.

When I had ascertained that Fred was really serious about going into management, I went to the section in his performance review which put on the record what a man's career objectives were, and what plans he had for reaching them. I asked Fred how he planned to become a manager. In response, he pointed out that he had a good track record as a project leader and had good relations with people in the plant. Besides, he had a lot of experience in all the operations of the company, and he personally thought that he was as good or better than many persons already in management.

I told him that I would not argue about his aptitude for managerial work. In fact, I felt that he was a good candidate for a management position, but would stand a better chance of getting such a position if he prepared himself for it. I told him how I had once been catapulted into management because I was the only degree engineer on the job, rather than for any particular managerial skills that I had. I tried to learn some of these on the job but most of them I learned by taking courses, going to seminars and by reading books. I found out that there were a lot of management skills I didn't know beans about through my education as an engineer. In the light of my experience, I saw clearly how a person could prepare himself for a management career. Some experience in management is important as well, but one person's experience is very limited. One of the biggest causes of career limiting is for a high quality specialist to be promoted into management and then fail to do the job. Some survive, but many are demoted or leave the organization with their tails between their legs.

Fred and I together developed a list of some special skills that he could acquire before moving up to management. These were the skills of delegation; interviewing techniques; preparation of budgets; understanding and interpretation of annual reports; financial principles; marketing principles; inventory control; personnel practices; etc. Fred got the point and enrolled in a night school course in general management. Within a year, he had moved into a technical supervisor's job outside the engineering department. His capacity as a manager increased so that within ten years he had moved up in the company to an executive position—which was one level higher than the one I had myself!

WHAT YOU WILL GAIN FROM THIS CHAPTER

Few people develop their mental capacities to maximum level. Many people stop their education when they leave school, not realizing that getting ahead depends on the ability to do things, as well as the determination to get ahead. Those who do develop their capacity to do more with the mind are sure to get ahead and get recognition in the long run. This chapter will help you to understand your limitations and assets as a human being. It will give you guidance on the most efficient way to develop your abilities and also the best ways to use the ones you already have.

BENEFITS FROM LEARNING TO USE THE INPUT-OUTPUT PRINCIPLE

1. You will identify the skills, know-how, and knowledge that you need the most to get ahead by being able to accomplish more.
2. You will know which are the most effective input and output means of human beings.
3. You will understand the relationship of education to job accomplishment and not be sidetracked into knowledge for its own sake.

In this chapter, you will learn about the Input-Output Principle which comes from system theory. It has been used effectively for years by system analysts for their computer modeling of the information flow in complex organizations. This Input-Output Principle is also effectively used in many branches of engineering. Recently it has become one of the accepted methods of management itself. Now we will apply it to the management of time.

In this chapter are specific ways you can save time by improving your input and output effectiveness. At the end of the chapter there will be guidelines which will enable you to put the principle to use for your own personal benefit.

THE INPUT-OUTPUT PRINCIPLE

Consider yourself, for the moment, to be a little black box whose contents are mysterious and wonderful, but unknown. Into the one end of the black box goes information, ideas, money, encouragement, etc., and out the other end comes good decisions, new information, better ideas, spoken wisdom, written words, works of art and so forth. You are indeed a very busy black box. You can do all kinds of clever things, but with the Input-Output Principle it is not necessary to know exactly what goes on in the little black box. What is important are the outputs we get from the inputs that go into it. This is known as the transformation. Time is saved if the transformation is efficient.

An example of a black box transformation is the case of a set of numbers which are put into it and come out the sum, or product, or some other mathematical result. That's one example of a transformation from inputs to outputs. Inside the black box may be a mechanical or electronic calculator. If it is efficient, you do not really care. Another good example is the matter of translation—input English, output French.

Cooking is something different in transformations. The outputs are much more imaginative and worth a lot more than the inputs. In go the ingredients, know-how, time and energy; out come the most wondrous things—which by the way, are only valued by those people who are hungry. This brings me to another point. Output must be useful to somebody in some situation in order for the black box to have a valuable transformation. For example, you may be able to output the most creative music, but if your employers output is iron castings then your particular output will not be valued by him. No utility.

We can break down our transformations of outputs from inputs into three categories:

1. At the *skill level*, are things that you learn to do. A handyman can make a rack of tools for his garage and that is something he can learn to do from a book or from a friend.

2. The *semi-professional level* of a tradesman or a technician involves learning *how to do and how to evaluate*. At this level one is able to judge the quality of the transformation as well as execute it. A craftsman knows when he is doing a good job. An amateur does not.

3. At the *professional level*, a person *plans, chooses among alternatives*, and *evaluates the result*. At this level you have the doctor who is given a problem, chooses among possible remedies and then evaluates the result. If the first drug doesn't work, you can go back and get another one (usually). A professional is dealing with uncharted areas and is able to use his mental capacity in an intelligent, problem-solving process. He or she may not be perfect, but has a high batting average.

From here on we consider mainly the mental transformations that take place in this black box. Physical transformations are most important in non-managerial jobs. They may even happen to be important to your life style, but not so important as the outputs which are valued by the organization you work with. The mental transformations are those that you make as a high order of animal species. This ability is what makes you valuable as a black box. A creative mental transformation is the highest level of human output. A single idea can be worth millions of mundane outputs. (Some of the creative aspects of time management were covered in chapter 5.)

Consider the ways in which inputs reach the black box. All inputs come through the senses. These senses are hearing, seeing, smelling, etc. Your main output means are speaking and writing. A more exhaustive list follows.

WAYS TO TAKE INPUTS AND MAKE OUTPUTS

INPUTS	OUTPUTS
Hearing	Speaking
Seeing	Writing
Smelling	Drawing
Tasting	Gestures
Touching	Eye Movements
Pressure Sensing	Body Odor
Heat Sensing	Body Heat
Vibration Sensing	Body Posture
Kinesia (position of limbs)	Position of Limbs
Accelerating (change of position)	Proximity to Other Persons
	General Appearance

There are several important limitations on you as a black box. Firstly, if you are listening, you can really only comprehend words as fast as a person speaks, which is only about 100 words per minute, whereas, it is easy to read 300 words per minute. Therefore, printed words can be taken as an input at three times the rate with the eyes than with the ears. Learning by pictures is even faster—in some cases a thousand times faster.

The second limitation occurs on the output. We give out mainly through speaking or through writing and drawing. There is no counterpart to seeing. In other words, we cannot send out the mental pictures we have in our minds. We must describe them and this takes a long time. Even if we draw, it is nowhere as rapid as acquiring the image in the first place.

From a utility point of view, the output of your black box is what is valued. What you do with your voice, your pen, your typewriter, your eye movements and your body movements, are the results of the transformations going on in the black box. Our input devices are much more efficient than the output devices. In an hour you can take in with the eyes what would take you years to describe in detail. However, inputs are not paid for by employers. It's the condensation, analysis or rearrangement of these inputs as new and creative outputs that are valued. So, what we need to look at is how we can use our brain to manipulate the many inputs into useful outputs.

THE INPUT-OUTPUT PRINCIPLE

By your mental capacity as a human being you transform selected inputs into useful outputs. Your senses carry enormous quantities of inputs to the mind which then must transform them into limited but useful outputs. You can improve the quality and quantity of your outputs by developing your mental capacity to the limit of your human potential.

SMART WAYS TO BECOME MORE EFFECTIVE

Improve Your Means of Input when Reading

The eyes are an efficient input device when used for reading. Most people are not trained to read at anywhere near their comprehension rate. That is, most people read at about 200 words per minute, which is only slightly better than speaking rate. Through training, most anyone can learn to read 600 words per minute. That is **three times as fast**. There is no loss in comprehension. Speed-reading tests show that there is an increase in comprehension. Learn how to speed-read.

As you can well believe, it is not only how **fast** you read that counts but **what** you read. So, let us consider what you can do under various circumstances to be more efficient in reading and thereby save time.

6 WAYS TO SPEED UP YOUR USEFUL INPUT FROM READING

1. Be selective. Ask yourself, "Would I have ordered this thing to read?" If not, throw it out, or at least set it aside for scanning when you are not busy.

2. If you are interested in the material, scan it first. Read over the index, abstract, the beginning and ending paragraphs. Is it still what you want to read?

3. Skip and skim. Usually an article or a book contains much material that you have read before and understand quite well. With business reading, you do not read from cover to cover like a novel. You decide what is worth reading by skipping and skimming each page or chapter. You pick out the important parts that are worth reading in some detail. You can skip and skim a whole book by looking at subtitles, keywords and figures. The skipping and skimming is particularly useful for business persons who are well-informed in their field and looking for additional information. Your time is well spent only when you get information which is useful and an addition to what you already have.

4. When you read: speed read. This is a technique best learned from an instructor. Nearly every community has classes in speed reading for adults. You can learn it in a few weeks. Since it is a remedial type of learning, it's helpful if the instructor has machines or other aids that help you scan line-by-line. There are also comprehension tests that you can use to increase your speed without losing comprehension. If you can't attend an organized class

with equipment, then there are books with exercises in them that help the ambitious reach new levels in reading speed.

5. Select, scan, and vary the speed. Some material can be read fast and some should be read slowly, particularly if it is new material to you. So the skilled reader of a book or article will first scan and select what is to be read and then vary the speed of reading according to the type of material.

Increasing your ability to read as an input device is not just seeing words. You must learn new knowledge to develop a new ability. There is more knowledge available than you can possibly ever learn by reading. Therefore, you must choose what it is you want to learn.

Improve Your Means of Input by Listening

Listening is another means of input. There is even a book called *Are You Listening?* Would you believe that there are seminars on how to listen? When you get right down to it, how many people really know how to listen? We listen by doing 90% of the talking.

Most people are completely unaware that they are often impeding the person with information to give. Listening is a skill, and you can become better at it.

If you feel that you wish to improve your ability to listen effectively, *learn to wait in silence* and not be embarrassed by an awkward pause in the conversation. You are receiving information and the other party needs time to collect his thoughts. He will fill in the awkward pause. This is a skill you can learn by yourself.

Learn about *non-verbal clues* such as persons nodding their heads when saying yes, clenching their fists in anger, and a lot of not-so-obvious things. You can learn this by observing people.

There are two components to listening, that is, hearing

the words people say, and understanding the meaning. Often the two are different, and non-verbal clues help you to know what to believe and what is important.

You have heard the expression of "a person talking in circles." Often the meaning is not in the words but in some hidden meaning in the overall structure of what is said. This is called the *meta-talk*. Learn about this, too.

Improving Your Output When Speaking

Speaking is one of the important output devices. Most executives and managers know that public speaking is an asset and usually find their way into some training if they need it. The trouble with public speaking courses is that they tend to emphasize formalism in speech. This is OK for the platform when you have a large audience, but it is not appropriate for office conversations. In a small group conversation, being natural is important but be sure to articulate clearly so that you are not misunderstood.

Here are some tips about making effective use of your speaking ability.

TIPS FOR EFFECTIVE OUTPUT WHEN SPEAKING

1. Be natural in small groups.
2. Employ the Threshold and Saturation Principle outlined in a previous chapter. Do not under-communicate, and do not over-communicate.
3. Augment your speaking with visual aids such as gestures and pictures. Remember that your receiver's eyes are his most powerful input device and a picture, in many cases, is truly worth a thousand words. On the average, people learn 83% by seeing.
4. Learn to dictate with some skill.

When you dictate, pause at the end of sentences. Dictate any special punctuation, and the start of a new paragraph. Many persons fail to learn how to use dictating equipment because they fail to discipline themselves for a few hours of training in how to do it. Actually, many men who dictate directly to their secretaries are guilty of showing-off and grandstanding. They may please their ego, but they are wasteful of their secretary as a resource person who could be helping with delegated work instead of scribbling shorthand.

Improve Your Output when Writing

Writing is the use of kinesia as an output device. You may read several books and then some magic transformation goes on in your mind, the end result of which is 100 precisely written words. While *what* you write is the most important thing, *how* you write can save you time in the long run, so here are a few tips.

SAVE TIME ON HANDWRITING

1. Write large if your handwriting is not clear. Leave spaces between the lines for corrections. Use a dark ink or dark lead pencil.

2. How fast can you write? I can write 40 words a minute in a style legible to my secretary. If it's for someone else to read, you and I can only do about 10 words per minute, and that is not very fast.

3. Write without looking—if you can. This is handy for blackboards because you do not cover what you are writing and it's good for taking notes at meetings.

4. Don't write! Dictate. With an effort, you might get your writing speed up to 40 words per minute but you can easily learn to dictate 100 words per minute and this is 2 ½ times as fast. Human beings are very inefficient output devices. Our words can't keep up with our thoughts and our fingers can't keep up with our words. So why make things worse than they are?

The portable pocket-size dictating machine is becoming an important asset to many managers and executives. Besides dictating most of the letters, they also dictate notes to themselves. They summarize interviews and meetings immediately afterwards and put them in their record. They record ideas as they flash through their minds.

Overcome any shyness that you have about dictating in a public place and you will make a lot better use of your waiting time. Much of this book has been dictated while waiting in airports or riding on airplanes. If the dictating machine has one fault, it is that it doesn't tell you that you are rambling on and getting disorganized. To avoid this, write out a brief outline or headings of what you are going to dictate when it is more than a short letter.

IMPROVING MENTAL TRANSFORMATION OF INPUTS TO OUTPUTS

You should realize by now, after reading about this principle, that what goes on in that black box of yours is an important part of your ability. You can improve your input-output devices, but in the long run it is the "wheels that turn around inside" that are paramount.

You acquired ability because you learned how to do things. (We are thinking mainly of mental transformations now.) Your specific occupation will require you to reach certain abilities and to keep improving them. Those are things you can best decide upon. What I wish to draw your attention to now are those general things that almost any executive and manager should consider in order to get recognition and get ahead.

1. The specific *jargon and technical language* of your occupation depends somewhat on the organization you are working with. You must spend a little time to be conversant with not only the spelling of these words, but what they really mean in the context of your organization. As you move up in management, you take over other units that you are

not familiar with. For example, a financial executive may move into general management where the engineering manager reports to him. In such a situation, the faster the financial person learns the engineering jargon, the better will be his communications and understanding with his subordinate manager in engineering. When we learn about other disciplines and specialties, we not only learn the jargon and technical language, but we tend to reduce the favorable bias we may have towards our own specialty. Even when we don't have a bias, we can be easily accused of it if we don't understand the basics. So, the executive who came up from engineering will probably take a seminar on finance for non-financial executives; the financial person will find a book that tells what engineering is all about.

2. *Basic English* is getting to be a problem in most organizations. The quality of this aspect of education has dropped off so badly that young persons coming into the organization are unable to compose grammatically correct sentences, or even to spell correctly. This means the executive who leaned on his secretary or subordinates for well-prepared material, is now going to have to learn to do it for himself. Good English is not just grammar and spelling. It is understanding of the logic that is built into the language. Knowledge of this logic improves a person's ability to express himself, and also to think.

The problem in basic English is real. It is attested to by the fact that many large organizations have short internal courses on letter writing and report writing. Unfortunately, these courses do not reach the executive level—and the problem may be yours. When an executive finds that his use of the English language as an output means is inadequate, he would be well advised to get some personal coaching, as night school courses tend to be rather slow.

Multi-Disciplinary Education is the new thing in management. As a matter of fact, management *is* multi-disciplinary. It includes elements of psychology, sociology, economics and philosophy. Managers who got their promotion because they made a good showing in one discipline often possess a narrow view of management. Many engineers who want to move up in management are now going back to school to take a Master of Business Administration (MBA) degree. This broadens their perspective and makes them able to do a good job at the executive level. There is also a field now called Management Science. It is the application of mathematics and computers to assist managers to handle complexity.

GUIDE YOURSELF TO TIME MASTERY

THE INPUT-OUTPUT PRINCIPLE

Through your mental capacity you transform selected inputs into useful outputs. Your senses carry enormous quantities of inputs to the mind which then must transform them into limited but useful outputs. You can improve the quality and quantity of your outputs by developing your mental capacity to the limit of your potential.

INPUTS ⟶ "BLACK BOX" TRANSFORMATION ⟶ OUTPUTS

Main Points
1. You can think of yourself as a "black box" that transforms inputs into useful outputs.
2. Your eyes are your most efficient means of input.
3. Your means of delivering outputs is not very efficient but can be improved.
4. The mental transformations that you make can be improved by intensive short courses and seminars.

DO THESE AND BECOME MORE EFFECTIVE

1. Refer to the input list in Table I. Which of these are important in your job? In your personal life. Pick the important ones and consider: Are they working well in the physical sense? Do you tend to use the inefficient input of hearing when you could be more effective by seeing? (i.e., listening vs. reading). Consider seriously your ability to speed-read. Read a newspaper passage for five minutes and calculate your words per minute. Less than 200 words per minute is way below your capacity. Six hundred is quite good. If reading fast is important to your occupation or life style, plan to become a speed-reader.

2. Refer to the output list in Table I. Which of these are important in your job? In your personal life? Can you benefit from any skill improvement in these? Check what has been suggested for speaking and writing.

3. Will your mental transformations be good enough for your desired position in two years? Now is the time to start on further education which will improve your ability to accomplish more. Review the suggestions listed under "Improving your Mental Transformations of Inputs to Outputs." Aim at developing your mental ability to its maximum potential.

14 | Techniques for Managing Time Spent On New Projects

KEY IDEA
You save time in the long run when you review and revise frequently in the early phases of a new project—using the Revision Principle.

The way to win on a large project is the same today as it was a century ago. Consider these two projects of the past, and what we can learn from them.

Project Chicago: A hundred wagons, loaded with provisions and families, followed by herds of horses and cattle, set out from Chicago on a gigantic migration through uncharted prairies and deserts. Two years later a few survivors reach the west coast. What started out as a gigantic project ended up as a disaster in Death Valley.

Project Virginia: About the same time a large migration went out of Virginia towards the far west. It was led by someone like Daniel Boone. A scouting party was sent ahead to test out various routes and passes which were weeks ahead of the major wagon train. When they were in difficult territory, the scouts sent back for an advance wagon party to see if they could get one wagon through the pass. If it didn't work they would try another route. They avoided having a major disaster. They reviewed plans and they revised. When the major party moved through, the trail was fairly well charted. Although they had some problems, the overall project was termed a success.

What is the lesson from history? The "project" from Virginia took a little longer at the beginning and it took a willingness to plan and revise. It involved waiting while alternatives were explored, but in the long run it turned out better than the Chicago project. The lesson we can learn is discussed in this chapter.

WHAT YOU WILL GET FROM THIS CHAPTER

You will learn how to save time on projects which are new to you, particularly on long-term and large-scale projects—by use of the Revision Principle. Examples of the Revision Principle are developed in this chapter. They are: to rebuild an organization; enter a new sales territory; enter a foreign market; develop a new product; market a new service—any major undertaking that is new to you and involves some risk.

By using the Revision Principle you will reduce the risk of expensive revisions or outright failure of a project nearing completion. You will know the best strategy to get to a new goal when the route is uncharted.

This chapter is unlike many of the previous chapters which dealt with specific ways to save time on short-term tasks or on routine activities. This chapter pertains more to your creative output; to your major job function; to the dynamic of your job; to what you are supposed to change for the organization.

When you are thinking about doing something new, it is best to have an overall plan or strategy. Given a good strategy, you will avoid those expensive losses of time and money which come about because a long term project was not properly launched. When you plan with the use of the Revision Principle you will avoid wasting resources. You will make a good showing in your organization if you understand and follow through with the guidelines at the end of this chapter.

THE REVISION PRINCIPLE

Imagine yourself today as a member of a project with a gung-ho leader who says, "This is the way we are going to go!" Two years later there are enormous overruns in cost and time and nothing really works out well. Even though the leader is replaced—perhaps several times—a salvaged project is never as good as one that started out well.

If you are going to lead a new project into uncharted territory, would you not rather be the Daniel Boone type? **You will probe; you will explore; you will build models and test them. You will try and predict what is up ahead.** The more you explore, probe, test, review and revise, the better the chances of a successful project. This is what the Revision Principle is all about.

You can have an expensive, unplanned revision that nobody wants, occurring late in the project,—or you can plan to have formal reviews and revisions early in the project, when you can get information on what lies ahead at a very low cost. Although this process **seems to delay** the project, in most cases it is **really easing the way** for the final success.

Consider the introduction of a very new product. When things are put together, be they electrical components, mechanical components, chemicals, or ideas, there is an interaction between them that is not very predictable. The problems will be downstream (time-wise) in the project unless they are discovered upstream.

It makes sense to assemble prototypes of new products, sales plans, reports, etc., and test them out before going into full scale implementation. You discover all kinds of things that give you information about what might have happened if you had gone directly to implementation. It may cause you to go back to the drawing board; it may make you start over again; or it may even make you scrap the project. These are "informal revisions" which are caused by the development of new information in the course of the project. It is only natural that some information comes about during the life of a project because it is impossible to predict it all beforehand. If you get this new information and put it to use, then it is a highly desirable thing to do. Therefore one should realize that *revision is both normal and desirable* on a new kind of project.

Given that revision is both normal and desirable, when is the best time to do it? Revisions at the beginning of a project are generally on paper or on inexpensive scaled down models or prototypes. Revisions at the end of a project involve a lot of resources and are expensive. Therefore it makes sense to plan to have early revisions while you are upstream in a project. This logic gives us the Revision Principle.

THE REVISION PRINCIPLE

It is better to have planned revisions upstream than to have unplanned downstream revisions which are costly in time and money.

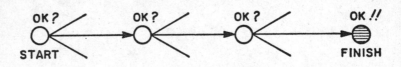

A PERFECT PROJECT IS A MYTH—A CASE HISTORY

I well remember the first time I learned about the importance of revisions. It happened on an engineering project, but what I learned has helped me with many non-technical projects. I had just joined a firm which had put me in charge of the television engineering department. Over the next few weeks their troubles unfolded before me and I was expected to apply some mysterious healing salve that was going to make everything right. A previous television design had given much field trouble, and now the whole of the finished warehouse stock was going through production once again. This time production was reworking them to a modified design which was supposed to end all their troubles. I asked for test results as proof that the modified design would be OK but there were none. Only blind hope. As it turned out we never ceased to be hounded for field improvements to that design. Looking back, we would have done well to scrap the whole project and all the TV sets produced therefrom. We wasted a lot of time trying to patch up a project that was poorly launched.

All the same, it did teach me something about new projects—never rush into implementation with a project that has not been tested out beforehand because *revisions in the implementation phase are very expensive and very limited in scope.*

After a few years, we worked out a good plan of *formal reviews and revisions* which generally resulted in successful projects on new things. You should skip over the technical aspects of this example, but note how we planned the formal reviews and revisions. The first design phase was on paper. Calculations were performed. Then a "breadboard" of the design was put together on wood and metal supports with wires holding it together. This tested out the basic idea. After the bugs were shaken out of this breadboard, we would review it and go to a handmade prototype which was very much like a production unit. After the prototype was completed and tested, and the engineering drawings issued for final production, we constructed six revised units to the final design drawings. These were put together by experienced production workers. *Everyone's advice was taken seriously and all necessary revisions were then put into the design* in time to be incorporated in the following pilot run of 100 units. The 100 units were field tested thoroughly, and the results reviewed. Any further revisions found to be warranted were put into the design just before full-scale production.

It would be wrong to assume that full-scale production was without some problems. Any major project has a few unforseen problems. But, by our process of formal upstream review and revision, we had shaken the major bugs out of the project before full-scale production took place.

I have applied the Revision Principle in many non-technical aspects such as: management studies; course development; article writing; and even in the writing of this book. It works just great. It continues to surprise me how smoothly a new project goes at the end when I have planned upstream revisions. Wasted time on downstream revisions is virtually eliminated.

SEVEN WAYS TO MAKE THE REVISION PRINCIPLE SAVE TIME FOR YOU

1. *Delegate a New Job in Progressive Phases*

When delegating something new to a subordinate which is uncharted territory for that person, then you should *take time to delegate it by progressive phases which permit you to review and revise.* This means that you take advantage of what most teachers do in school when teaching a new subject. You first give the overall picture. Then you elaborate this with examples and reiterate the concept or principle. All the time you check with your subordinate to see that his mental model and your mental model are coming closer together. In other words, you are testing the delegate to see if what he knows is what you have taught him. If it is not, then you reiterate and build a revised picture with more examples and more analogies. *By investing a little time in checking and revising, you reduce the risk that your time will be wasted later by a misunderstanding.*

2. *How to Enter an Unknown Sales Territory*

If your organization wants to expand its sales, don't allow it to jump into unknown territory with all the resources and power at its disposal. Send out some scouts to chart a way first. We will consider an "unknown" sales territory to be one where either a new kind of product is involved or there is a new kind of customer.

ENTERING AN UNKNOWN SALES TERRITORY

1. Send out a scout, say the sales manager, to talk to people in the territory who are selling similar things. He looks around for potential dealers, distributors, or customers but makes no specific moves.

2. Enlarge the penetration by sending out an advance party of salesmen. They may be contracted to test the market for a limited time period.

3. Have a review meeting and lay on some more elaborate plans. You may wish to open up some new offices and facilities that require considerable capital. You can get outside opinions and compare them with your own to make sure that you are not being led down the garden path by your own enthusiasm.

4. Make your final moves in a planned orderly fashion—Phase 1, Phase 2, Phase 3, until you can say that everything is going fine. Then hand it over to the regular operating branch of the organization.

3. *When Introducing a New Service—Test a Small Region First*

A service is something that people like to have on a continuing basis. You must be above the threshold value, or not there at all. In other words, revisions on market testing for a service below the threshold level, must be interpreted with care. The lack of a positive result may be not negative, but simply that you have not passed the threshold value. Therefore *it is best for a service to concentrate in a small area* where the service can be above the threshold value. Look for the customers to return and use the service again. If it's good, you can go on to a larger test. If it's not good, you can take a small loss and "go back to the drawing board."

Look upon introducing a new service as being like opening up a new pizza parlour. You can't ship in pizzas by parcel post and get the business going. The threshold value is one rented store with service equal to what the competitors are able to give. You can see it's better to try out one store than to try out a hundred. It may delay the buildup a bit but it also reduces the risk of an enormous failure.

4. *A Plan for Training Salesman on a New Product*

Suppose your salesmen must learn about an absolutely new product. It will not just be another leaf in their sales folder. They must learn in detail what the new features are; how it works; what kind of customers buy; and why they buy. We are talking about something like an outboard motor company going into the business of selling all-terrain vehicles. You can imagine a sales training program as follows:

A PLAN TO TRAIN SALESPERSONS ON A NEW PRODUCT

1. A letter announcing the entry into a new product line and the benefits that will ultimately accrue to the sales persons.
2. A brochure which describes the new products and the new market in a general way.
3. Demonstrations of the new product, either at a sales meeting or in the field with the salesman. Test comprehension of new products. Revise steps 2 and 3 if indicated.
4. Assign a pilot team to practice selling interviews under the guidance of a coach.
5. Examine sales results. If poor, repeat step 4.
6. If pilot result OK, go out to the field and sell, sell, sell.

5. Rebuild an Organization with Planned Phases

It is likely in the career of a manager-executive that at one time he or she will be put in charge of a new department which must be rebuilt from the bottom up to the top. However you just can't go in, fire everybody, and bring in new staff, because operations must continue. Instead, you move in and try to find out what's going on. There will be some talented people in the organization who are just waiting to be given a chance. There will be some meatheads who have surely got to be demoted or shown the door. There may be some persons who do not have the qualifications to do the kind of job that is now required of them—this often happens when a new technology is introduced.

You cannot rebuild an organization overnight. You must do it in phases. These are the phases that should be involved.

PHASES TO REBUILD AN ORGANIZATION

1. A diagnostic phase where you find out what is really going on without disturbing the ongoing operations.

2. A trial reorganization phase where the people with apparent potential are given acting positions to see if they can really perform. This is a test and you can go back to step 1 or go on to 4 without losing the time an error in promotion would cost you.

3. An implementation phase where you bring in new blood, new knowledge, and additional resources at all levels to beef up those areas which have been found wanting in your diagnosis. Take the time needed to recruit and train good people. You will avoid the time wasted by hasty decisions.

4. A consolidation phase where the new organization is shaped up and expected to produce results. The incompetents are weeded out, the deadwood given jobs they can do, and the new blood is given all the authority it needs to get results.

5. A vacation phase. You earned it, you deserve it, and you need it.

6. Careful Induction of a New Employee will Shorten the Time to Produce Results

You hire people because you need them as a resource. But in professional and managerial positions the new resource does not begin to perform overnight. If you want them to perform well and do it reasonably soon, then you must have an induction program. This may appear to delay the productive point but in the long run it will reduce hiring disasters.

I personally don't like the "sink-or-swim" attitude that is often used with new employees. It takes considerable effort to recruit and select a person in a managerial or professional field. This effort should continue for some period after the person has arrived on the site. The induction procedure that I have used for employees is as follows:

NEW EMPLOYEE PRODUCTIVITY COMES FASTER THIS WAY

1. Introduce the person to all the key people in the organization with whom he or she will ultimately come into contact, including those several layers up. This may be the only time the new person talks with the chief executive of the organization for many years to come.

2. Take time out for a long interview to deal with any concerns the employee has developed since agreeing to take the job. Now the person has the job, he may ask some embarrassing questions which would have prevented him getting the job had he asked them earlier. Now is the chance to start the open door policy.

3. Shepherd the person around for a few days so that they learn the routine of coffee breaks and lunches; or assign a subordinate to do this.

4. Pamper your new employee a bit. He or she is in a strange place and this may be the only time you can

afford the luxury of pampering. You can give him hell-firo later on when he has done something to deserve it.

5. Check out your new employee's performance frequently enough to find out if your induction needs follow up by training in job skills.

7. A Strategic Plan Needs Milestone Checkpoints

There should be something about your job that changes. This is the dynamic of the job. Something grows or something diminishes. In order to make it change in the way it should, you must do some strategic planning. This is long-term thinking about what is the best general policy and what are the best kinds of decisions—rather than making specific day-to-day decisions. It's a look at the future, to where your organization wants to be in 5, 10, or 15 years. In some organizations, planning is so poor that even one year ahead would be strategic planning.

Whatever they are, new things don't come about suddenly or by themselves. It is best to bring about these changes with planned phases of review and revision. These are moves in the right direction from which you can pull back if things don't go quite as planned.

Strategic planning is not just the setting of objectives and goals, but a planning of revision and review points as

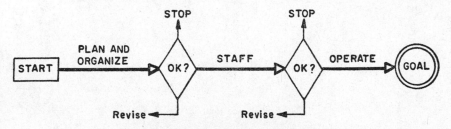

Milestone Checkpoints for Review and Revision

Figure 14-1: A Strategic Plan

milestones along the way. By having a **formal plan with milestone checkpoints**, you will have a good chance of arriving there. Otherwise you may just have a document with the label "Strategic Plan"—which dies of neglect in a file.

OBTAINING THE BENEFITS OF USING THE
REVISION PRINCIPLE

You can best make use of the Revision Principle when you have a long-term project which includes new work for you; or you are seeking the solution of some kind of "fuzzy" problem. Consider its use whenever you go into "uncharted territory." The intelligent way to use the Revision Principle is to plan to have additional formal reviews and revisions while upstream in the project and thereby avoid expensive ones downstream.

GUIDE TO TIME MASTERY

THE REVISION PRINCIPLE

It is better to have planned revisions upstream than to have unplanned downstream revisions that are costly in time and money.

Main Points
1. Review and revision is normal and desirable.
2. Upstream revision costs the least in time and money.
3. By planned, upstream revision, you reduce the risk of lost time downstream.

Guidelines to Mastering the Revision Principle

1. What is the main thing that you are trying to bring about by your job? Think about the changing aspect of your job. What is to be different in the years ahead? Can this difference benefit from having more planned reviews and revisions in the upstream phase of a strategic plan? If so, make such a plan. It will save you time in getting there.

2. Do you have any subordinates on long-term projects which would benefit from the use of the Revision Principle? If so, direct them into planning out the formal reviews and revisions that they should have in a project.

3. Is your organization as a whole making use of the Revision Principle or is it collecting too many disasters that could have been prevented? Do you have a responsibility to pass along the principle of planned reviews and revisions? If so, you should do so and save your organization some of that non-renewable resource—time.

15 | How to Experience the Sheer Joy of Accomplishment

KEY IDEA
By having check points along the way, you will feel good about your progress towards what you want—using the Milestone Principle.

J.P. was a manager in a Los Angeles aircraft firm who appeared to be failing in the job which sustained him. He came in regularly and put in the required hours, but he lacked the pep and enthusiasm that he had shown five years ago when he was first promoted into management.

J.P. himself felt that he wasn't getting anywhere in his career and that his work was no longer as good as it used to be. He attributed this to the bleak outlook for the aircraft industry, and had developed a "what's-the-use" attitude.

Even if this rationale satisfied J.P., it certainly didn't satisfy his boss. He was called in for a special performance review and told that his performance had slipped way below what he was capable of doing. If he didn't pull himself out of his lethargy he would go into a nose-dive and would not have a job after the end of the current project.

This seemed to convince J.P. that what he thought was true. Instead of checking up on himself, he went into a period of depression.

Fortunately for J.P., because of his visible depression, he was referred to an industrial psychologist. What was happening to J.P. was what is generally known to psychologists as "the middle-aged career crisis." At this point in life, a man who has tried to get somewhere realizes that he has gotten just so far, and that he is probably not going to go any further. After a bit of mental readjustment this crisis normally passes without any severe difficulty. In J.P.'s case, however, the crisis was accentuated by the fact that his future was going to be worse than usual if he didn't do something about it.

After a few hours of chatting, the industrial psychologist told J.P. about the middle-aged career crisis and J.P. started to seriously examine where he was going to go. For one thing he had set his sights on a high executive position early in life, and failing that at least he could have been president of his own company, or chairman of its board, or something like that. He now realized that this had been a mere fantasy because he had done nothing to make progress towards that goal. He had floated along on the stream of life. Because of having a good education, and a bit of luck in an expanding aircraft industry, he had moved up into a manager's position. He had done quite well for a "drifter," but not as well as he might have done had he made a step-by-step plan for achieving something on the executive ladder.

Let's leave J.P. and his problem and assume that things worked out reasonably well. Our interest at this point is to examine the causes of an apparent lack of enthusiasm by some people in their work. They become apathetic and they vegetate. They procrastinate and they feel fatigued. They just can't seem to get going on any project with enthusiasm. Somewhere, sometime in your career you are likely to feel this way. I have felt this way and triumphed over it—more than once. You can do the same.

WHAT YOU WILL GAIN FROM THIS CHAPTER

In chapter 3 you were shown how to make use of the Purpose Principle. It has been assumed that if you are a reader of this kind of book, you have a pretty good idea of what your purposes are. Now we will go deeper into the subject. After reading this book you may want to clarify your purposes. In any case, a clearer definition of your purposes coupled with some milestone planning will enable you to use them to motivate yourself to do your work enthusiastically. When you have defined your purposes in some written form and when you have milestones of achievement for getting there, then you will have control of your life and your time.

BENEFITS FROM USING THE MILESTONE PRINCIPLE

1. You will be able to enjoy doing much of your work.
2. You will not be listless.
3. You will be self-motivated.
4. You will experience the sheer joy of accomplishment.

In this chapter you will recognize expressions of common wisdom and learn some of the wisdom of the ages. It is agreed that setting objectives is important in life. Following that, there will be seven ways in which you can be specific about motivating yourself with milestone check points.

THE MILESTONE PRINCIPLE

At some future point in your life there will be a new state of affairs. Things will not be as they are now. They will be different because of changing circumstances, whether you make any plans or not. If you do make plans to achieve a specific state of affairs, there is a good possibility that they will be much to your liking.

In order to be able to work your way to a desired state of affairs, you must have some idea of what it should be like. You will probably start off with a mental image of what the future state of affairs should be, be it wealth, prominence, leisure, love or what have you. A mental image can be a good guide, but for most people a mental image might become a fantasy. Like the pot of gold at the end of the rainbow, it's a nice mental image but you can never get there.

A better way to describe a future state of affairs is to write a scenario about it. Write it the way it will be. Say: I will have such and such, and I will be doing this, and I will be in this place. One or two pages make a nice scenario. The advantage of having a written scenario is that you can review it and see whether it is realistic or just a fantasy. Once you have a written description or scenario of the future state of affairs, then you can improve the description by establishing objectives.

An objective is a statement of what is to be achieved. For example, you may say, "In five years I will have an equity of $50,000." You might have an objective: "In 20 years I will have raised a family of three children." These are objectives because they state what is to be accomplished at the end of a given period. They aptly describe the new state of affairs. Objectives do not state **how** you are going to get to the new state of affairs, but they state **what** the new state of affairs is to be. Let me explain. If you have an objective of $50,000 of equity, there are many, many ways to get there and that comes later on in your planning. If you state how you are going to get there in the objective, then you restrict yourself as to the means. In other words, the objectives are the ends, and not the means. So much for the new state of affairs. Let me explain what this description will do for you by a few examples.

Imagine that you are a person lost in the desert. There's nothing but cactus, sand, rocks, sun, and snakes. You don't feel very good while hiking but you have an image of your comfortable hotel. This will sustain you hour after hour and maybe for a whole day. But not forever. If you are sustained only by blind hope, or by a mirage of an oasis on the desert, you are bound to be discouraged in the end. Suppose, however, you come to a desert road which has a little sign that says, "Ten miles to the Desert Oasis Hotel." You gain some enthusiasm, but after a while your energy flags and you become a little apathetic. Then you see another sign that says, "Eight miles to the hotel," then five miles, three miles, and finally you are there. The lesson in the story is that two things together will give you energy to accomplish something. They are **a vision of the future and a set of milestone markers**.

A manager can have a clear picture of a future state of affairs which is commensurate with his or her capability. He can then mark off the appropriate milestones of accomplishment and progress through preparation and promotion to the top—provided of course that he is not too scared to make the moves. Like the man in the desert, if he didn't have the heart to start out on the 10-mile trip, he would never get there.

Man is distinguished from other animals in one peculiar way: he can visualize the future. Lower animals cannot. A dog that is lost in the desert cannot visualize that any new road has got something specific at the end. Blind hope and instinct is really all he has. Not bad for a dog; but not so good for a human being in a rat-race organization. It has been said that "Man is a goal-seeking animal." Be this as it may, you can see that milestones are necessary in order to provide the reward and motivation to get to that distant goal. It is important to connect up what you are doing right now with where you want to be later. Since the connection between what you are doing right now and the long-term objective may be remote, it is better to connect them up with some interim points which we shall call milestones. We are now ready to make a statement of the principle.

THE MILESTONE PRINCIPLE

> You will most likely work enthusiastically towards your purposes when you have a milestone plan to get there. You need to be able to connect what you are doing right now with a milestone on the road to where you want to be.

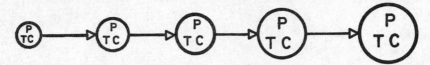

SAYINGS ABOUT FUTURE PLANNING

The Common Wisdom

"He doesn't know where he's going in life."
"He's just spinning his wheels."
"He has no purpose in life."
"If you don't know where you're going, you can't get there."

The Wisdom of the Ages

"No fair wind blows for a ship that has no port of destination," by Michel de Montaigne.
"Our todays and yesterdays are the blocks with which we build," by Henry Wadsworth Longfellow, in *The Builders*.

Syd's Wisecrack

A person without a milestone plan is like a fly buzzing on a window. There is an objective—but no intelligent plan to get there.

SIX STEPS TO A LIFETIME OF ACCOMPLISHMENT WITH THE MILESTONE PRINCIPLE

1. *Polish the Mental Image of What You Want*

Many people are sustained by a visual image of what they ultimately want. The pioneer who crossed the mountains and prairies and tilled the ground for years was sustained by the image of a pleasant little farmhouse under a shady tree. There are 3 attributes of a motivating mental image.

1. It is realistic.
2. It is feasible.
3. It is possible to have visual milestones of the route.

So visualize what you want in the future and polish it up in your mind.

2. Write Up Your Own Scenario

If you write down a description of the future state that you wish to achieve, you can call it a scenario. (The writing of alternative scenarios has been used frequently in technological forecasting.) It is best to write a number of scenarios and then select one which is both desirable and feasible. The advantage of the written scenario is that it gets one out of the area of fantasy. It can be shown to other people and they can make comments on ways to get there and its feasibility. A mental fantasy is not easy to discuss and check out with objective persons. A good scenario has the following attributes.

1. It has a specific date in the future.
2. It has a specific place in the future.
3. You are one of the actors.
4. It covers all aspects of your lifestyle.

3. Write Out Your General Objectives

An objective is a statement that states **what is to be achieved and not how it is to be achieved.** The focus is on achievement, that is, on the ends and not the means. It may take several objectives to describe a new situation. Here is a sample set of objectives which might suit the feasible aims of a person who is new in management.

1. To be a senior executive in charge of a company about the size of the one I'm in.
2. To achieve a salary range of $50-$80,000.

3. To have an independent income so that I can make bold decisions.

4. To have a career which is consistent with my personal objectives of having a happy home life with three children raised to successful maturity.

5. To have economic security for retirement.

6. To be healthy for most of my life and to live a long time.

You may note that some of these objectives are not fully consistent with the others. This gives rise to the tradeoff. There may be a tradeoff of success as an executive with time for a happy home life. We will talk about tradeoff ratings later. In the meantime note that the objectives are fairly general, and easy to subscribe to.

What makes your objectives useful is the elimination of other objectives. Quite clearly if you have an objective of going up the executive's ladder then you do not have an objective of being a monk with a vow of poverty, a freelance journalist, or a vacation resort owner.

Setting your objectives will call for some serious thinking about the future, what you really want to do, and what is possible. The thing that may be lacking in high level objectives is a set of milestones or short-term objectives, although it is possible to construct some. The milestones to being a senior executive are obvious—you must first reach the level above you. You can call this one your short-term objective and work towards it.

4. *Weight the Objectives.*

All objectives are not of equal importance. There will often be some tradeoff between them. The first step in deciding on the importance of objectives is to put them on cards. Then sort them into a stack in which the top ones are most important, and the bottom ones are the least important. It is helpful to separate out the long-term and the short-term objectives when doing this. Your long-term objectives may remain very stable while your short-term objectives change as the situation warrants. Once you have a list of the order of importance (called a rank ordered list), you can go to the weighting of the items.

Weighting objectives means assigning numbers to them according to their relative importance. If two objectives are of equal importance, give them the same number. You can take 100 points and spread them around among the objectives. Juggle some up and some down until you are satisfied. If you have used 100 points, then each of the objectives represents a percentage contribution to your overall purposes. In other words, to go back to the objectives in number 3, if being an executive, and having financial independence, each get 25 points, then each contributes 25% to the total.

5. Decide on the Optimum Projects to Get you There

Once you have a set of objectives you can develop some projects for achieving these objectives. This assumes of course that your objectives are not just to maintain the status quo, but to achieve some new and more desirable state for you. This desirable state is not likely to arise out of your ordinary work or just out of good luck. It will arise because of something you do for yourself. This is what I will call a project. A project is something special that you take on over and above your work and family obligations—in order that you can ultimately achieve a high-level objective.

First, you need a list of possible projects, and a description of what is to be achieved and how you are going to do it. You will know when you have finished, and be able to measure what you have done. This is part of the secret of motivating yourself to be enthusiastic about achieving your objectives. You need to have specific checkpoints so that you can see that you have accomplished something. You need to remind yourself that what you are working on serves some higher-level objective that you want in life. As you complete each project en route to your objective, you will get immense satisfaction and be able to go enthusiastically on to the next one.

Most likely you will not be able to do all of your project

ideas. Therefore it is important that you make a selection of the ones which will contribute the highest utility towards your purposes. This was discussed in chapter 4, but whereas you made a subjective evaluation of the utility of each activity or task, in this case I show you how to evaluate your projects quantitatively.

Once you have a set of weighted objectives that you believe in, then you can score the projects in a decision matrix as shown in Figure 15-1. You see a brief description of some of the objectives and their assigned weights. The weights have been divided by 100 so they will be convenient for calculation. This means that a weight of 25 points out of 100 now becomes a weight of .25. All of the weights should add up to 1.0. Take each project and consider how much it would satisfy each of your objectives. If it satisfies an objective very well then the score might be 90% to 100%. If it is so-so, or you are not sure, then the score would be 50%. If the contribution is modest it may only score 25%. The exact numbers you use are not important because it is your own scale and your own decision. You are only trying to compare one project with another. The entries in the boxes of the matrix are the percent of satisfaction obtained from the project when completed. When you have entered all of these percent satisfactions, multiply them by the weights and add them up. This is a weighted sum and is shown on the right of the box. An example of the calculation is at the bottom of the figure. **You choose to do the projects with the highest score.**

This is a very systematic way of deciding on projects for getting ahead. It seems like a lot of work but we are talking about a very serious matter. You reserve this for the important decisions in life. You cannot do all the projects, so you select the ones which have the best potential for benefitting you. Then you break them down into recognizable tasks which end at little milestones along the way to their completion.

PROJECTS / OBJECTIVES WEIGHTS	Become a Senior Exec.	Earn high income	Financial Independence	Happy home live	Health	Weighted Sum = % overall satisfaction
	.1	.3	.2	.2	.2	1.0
A. Buy 6-plex at Newburg	0%	10%	75%	50%	50%	38%
B. Take mgmt course at college	80%	80%	10%	50%	50%	54%
C. - - - - -						

Entries are the % Satisfaction of Objectives

Weighted Sum of B = .1x80% + .3x80% + .2x10% + .2x50% + .2x50%

= 8 + 24 + 2 + 10 + 10 = 54%

Figure 15-1: A Decision Matrix for Projects to Attain Your Objectives

6. *Experience the Sheer Joy of Accomplishment Every Day*

Every day you will have things you *must do* and *want to do*. Your routine work and life determine a good portion of what you *must do*, and your plan of optimum projects contains tasks which are part of what you *want to do*.

To enjoy what you do, you must reward yourself. There is no better reward than the one you can bestow on yourself by ticking off your completed daily tasks. You are rewarded even more when you reach a milestone of your project.

Here are two ways to experience the sheer joy of accomplishment:

1. Carry a priorities card with you, as shown in chapter 3 on the Purpose Principle. Mark the high priorities with three stars. Now, here is the important key—*cross them off as you do them.* This will reward you many times daily. Every time you start a new card you will realize how much you have actually accomplished! You will be amazed. I do it all the time.

2. If you work at one place most of the time, use a pile of 3×5 cards to list all of your tasks for the day. Sort them by priorities and put the highest priority on top. When you look at the top card, consider how you will accomplish it in the least time using some principle in this book—then do it. When done, snap it off the pile and toss it into a box of accomplished tasks—you will feel the exhilaration of a home run hit. (A highly productive acquaintance of mine likes to celebrate the end of a task by tearing up the card and throwing the pieces joyfully into his waste basket.)

OBTAINING THE BENEFITS OF THE MILESTONE PRINCIPLE

When?

If, at any point in your career you feel apathetic, lethargic, and don't seem to be getting anywhere, then it is time to replan. It's hard to get off your butt and do some serious planning when you are apathetic. But, paradoxically, that is when you need it the most. It will bring you out of your apathy.

What?

What you should do is make a list of long-term objectives, sometimes known as goals. These should state what is to be achieved, but not how to achieve it. You should also make sub-objectives, or milestones, which are feasible points to be reached and measured.

How?

How to make use of these objectives as motivators is up to you. I carry them on a small card in my notebook so that I can dangle the card in front of my nose once in a while and polish up my mental image. Some people plaster them all over the walls. That form of display has the advantage that once you let everyone know what your objectives are it is hard to back down.

The two important things about objectives are: they should be written down; and they should be used frequently to motivate you.

TIME MASTERY

Eventually, you will find that you have mastered time. No longer will it be your master. You will know what your purposes are; you will have a priorities list; and you will guide your activities by those things that contribute most to your objectives. You will also know clearly what you want to do. You will be applying the time mastery principles and techniques that you learned in this book regularly.

This book is organized so that you can go back easily to dig more gold out of the mines labelled "principles." The end of each chapter shows you how to apply the principle again and again. I always find it inspirational and challenging to think of a principle and find a new and exciting way to apply it.

The other way you can make further use of this book is

to use the Index of Time Tips. Suppose you are having some difficulty with telephoning; you will find many specific tips on telephones in the index. You can review them in the book and focus on the telephone time problem.

When you are the master of your time, you will feel good about it. You will want to share your time mastery secrets with others—and you will have the time to do it!

Appendix

Time-Saving Equipment, Devices and Forms

TELEPHONE

Hands-free Telephone

• A special telephone or an adapter for the one you have. It allows you to use your hands or move about your office while you communicate with the other party.

• You can make notes while you talk, write out an order, compose a confirming letter, etc. Others in your office can participate in the conversation.

• Units cost from $50 to $300, or may be rented from the telephone company.

• A shoulder-fitting device that clamps to your telephone handset will make you partially hands-free for under $5.

Telephone Headset

• An attractive and lightweight earphone and mouthpiece like the one switchboard operators use.

• Your hands can be free and the voice quality is tops. It can plug into your telephone set and give you the option of using the headset or your regular handset. Very nice for a person who uses the telephone almost continuously.

• If a secretary-typist has one of these, she can be transcribing a tape and switch over to the telephone when it rings. If a secretary takes many messages, she can save time by typing while she listens.

• Costs about $3 per month to rent from your telephone company.

Automatic Dialer

• A panel of buttons that sits beside the telephone handset. You push a button and a stored number is "dialed" quickly and accurately. Available with 15 to 80 buttons.

• Saves time when you or your secretary call the same number frequently. All the complicated digits for long-distance calls can be "dialed" by simply pushing the button opposite the name of the person you are calling. Frees you or your secretary for other work.

• Some models have a feature to store any number dialed by hand so that if a connection is not made, it can be "dialed" later by the push of a button—a great time saver for people who bungle up eleven-digit telephone calls.

• At least one such device is equipped to automatically re-dial a busy number up to 18 times, or until it is answered. It saves you time because you can be doing other light work while it tries to complete the call for you.

• Costs $50 to $300 to buy. You can rent one from the telephone company for about $10 per month. Being electronic, this equipment will come down in price and its storage capacity will increase.

PORTABLE TAPE RECORDERS

• Mini-cassette portable recorders are no larger than a shirt pocket and weigh about eleven ounces. They are easy to carry in pocket or purse.

• You save time because you can dictate letters, reports and ideas whenever you are waiting or travelling. You can also listen to tapes which educate or amuse you. See chapter 6 for "Thirteen Ways to Accomplish More With the Use of a Portable Tape Recorder".

• Costs $35 to $300 for a portable unit, plus $200 to $400 for good transcribing equipment. Prices are coming down as did the price of calculators.

TELEPHONE ANSWERING TAPE RECORDER

• A special tape recorder can be put on your telephone to take messages. With some you can get the messages by telephoning your number and interrogating it with a special code device.

• One way to get a spell of uninterrupted time is to tell your callers by this machine that you are "in conference with yourself and will call back after such-and-such time". Give an alternative number for urgent calls—and apologize, because some people hate these machines, even though they wish they could get some uninterrupted time themselves. (Naturally, a secretary or answering service can do this for you and apply some tact.)

• Costs $100 to $600, with expected price reductions because of its electronic nature.

PAGING SERVICE

• A small hand-size unit is carried with you and you are "paged" by a beeping sound, a vibration, or a light. This tells you to call in for a message. Some units can give you the message by radio. Rental and ownership services are available in most cities from telephone companies and equipment suppliers. The radio waves penetrate buildings and cars. Rural service and everywhere-service may eventually be available.

• Saves time because you can take action when it is important. You can also be at a meeting while waiting for an important telephone call. Great for salesmen, doctors and tradesmen. Now moving into executive suites. (Can be turned off while playing golf.)

ALARMS

Alarm Wrist Watch

• Available as a mechanical watch with a buzzer, or with digital read-out and a beeper. Usually water-resistant but not waterproof because of the holes for the sound to come out.

• Helps you remind yourself about timely actions such as meetings, appointments, returning telephone calls, etc. You avoid time wasted through forgetting. Also doubles as an alarm clock when you travel—or nap.

• Costs $25 and up. It is only carried by shops and catalogs with very complete lines.

Desk Alarm & Calculator

• A novel item about the size of a pocket calculator, intended for desk use. It can be programmed to beep at four separate times.

• You can be reminded to take timely action for four events in a day, such as: morning coffee; lunch; afternoon coffee; and quitting time!

• About $70 when first introduced. Look for interesting combinations of timers and other things in the future. Look also for calculators made to save time for people in special occupations.

Pocket Timer

• A watch-size timer on a key chain which is sold as a gift item to remind one to recharge the parking meter. Time settings of five minutes to two hours.

• Because this timer can be set for short times, you can use it to remind yourself that time is up on what you are doing. Use for meetings, telephone calls, and especially for making a presentation where you do not want to ramble on and on.

• Costs $3 to $10. Equally as useful is a kitchen timer with a bell alarm, although less portable.

A Novel Timer with a Tape Recorder

• Want to liven up a seminar-workshop? A meeting? A lunch call?

• A tape recorder can be your timer. First record silence for the period being timed. Then record a bugle, siren, whistle bell—whatever will get attention. What an effect you can create! You can record several intervals on one tape—up to one hour on one side.

• My mini-cassette portable tape recorder sounds a loud tone at the end of the tape. I use it as a 15-minute timer.

Electric Timer Switches

• A hand-size box that plugs into a wall outlet and shuts the power on and off. Its principal sale is for turning house lights on and off while owners are away.

• Useful for turning equipment on and off at the office. Do not waste a person's time when this device will save it. Turn on copying machines before starting time so no time is lost waiting for them to warm up.

• You will not worry about the coffee maker in the office if a timer shuts it off at quitting time.

• If you drive in northern winters, save energy on your block heater by turning it on while you sleep.

• Costs $10 to $20.

PRINTED FORMS

Diaries & Schedules

• Pocket and desk diaries are available in all sizes—for daily, monthly or yearly schedules. Some have places to write down your priorities list, reminders to telephone, expense records and so forth. Some have a convenient tab to tear off for each sheet so you can open the book easily to the current page.

• You accomplish more and save time by doing things when you plan to do them instead of at some inefficient time. Some persons have so many things to do that memory alone is not enough. Chapters 3 and 4 of this book show how to decide what to do and when to do it.

• Costs vary. A calendar is enough for some people. Some use a calendar pad as large as their desk pad. Some use wall charts costing a few dollars. Some managers and executives use separate monthly diaries which they review at the beginning of every day. The more elaborate sets cost about $25 per year.

Pre-printed Multiple-copy Memo Forms

• Two to four sheets are fastened together and have carbons in place. The senders name and address is printed on each. The sender writes or types a short message, keeps one form, and sends the rest to the recipient, who in turn uses one for the reply and one for a file copy. Some come with envelopes having windows that save addressing time.

• Great for short internal memos and some external correspondence. Time saved by not having to wait for typing.

• Costs from 2 cents to 15 cents for pre-printed forms and envelopes.

Telephone Message Pads

• Pre-printed with headings so that the message taker is prompted to get complete information from the caller.

• Time saved is greater for busy persons when the message

taker is prompted to get a brief message about the nature of the call so that the priority of returning the call can be established.

Transmittal Notices

• Pre-printed forms to clip or staple to something being sent to a colleague, or for circulation among your staff. Prepare and reproduce your own with a list of persons to whom you send things frequently. Add a checklist of actions you might expect such as "For your comments," "For your approval," "Take action," "Call me," "For your info," "Return," "File," "Sign," etc.

Project Record Folio

• A pocketed folder with overlapping record cards for each of the projects you are working on. It may have tabs for follow-up dates.
• Saves time when managing many projects or many persons with projects. You start your day by noting your follow-up tabs. In the folio are task and progress cards for those involved. You can also add new projects as they arise, and take out finished ones for the file.
• Costs $20 to $100.

COMPUTERS

Computer Conferencing

• A typewriter-like computer terminal connects you with a network of persons who have terminals on the same computer. The computer stores all messages until the recipient requests the computer to put all or part of them on his terminal. No special training is necessary.
• People save time by not having to travel to and from a meeting place. The meeting business takes place on an intermittent basis until completed. This is not for urgent meetings, but a viable replacement for some national meetings.

• Cost is currently about $10 per participant in a "meeting". Costs are coming down, as are most computer services.

Computer Search & Retrieve

• Printed words and numbers can be stored in a computer and rapidly scanned for analysis or retrieval.
• Abstracts of most scientific papers are stored on computers and can be searched for key-word combinations.
• Current company records of sales, expenses, profit, etc. can be stored on a computer. An executive or a secretary can get an up-to-date report or analysis from a computer terminal in the office.
• Costs coming down, but already within reach of office budgets.

THE OFFICE LAYOUT TO SAVE TIME

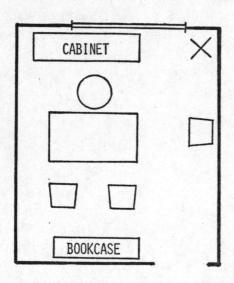

TRADITIONAL LAYOUT
- LIGHT OVER SHOULDER
- "BIG SHOT" APPEARANCE
- PERSONS APT TO LOOK
  IN DOOR & INTERRUPT

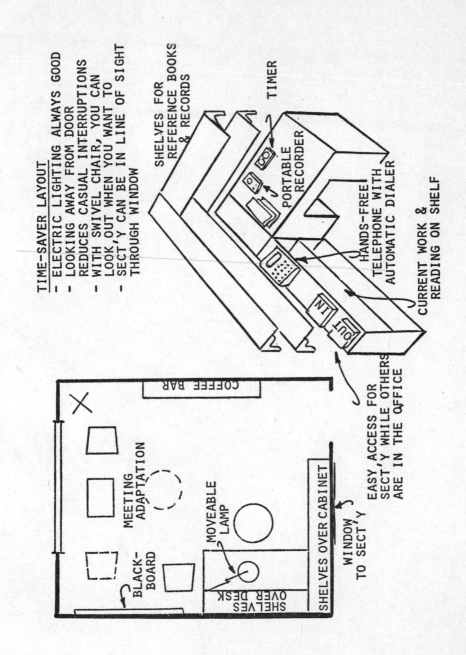

TIME-SAVER LAYOUT
- ELECTRIC LIGHTING ALWAYS GOOD
- LOOKING AWAY FROM DOOR
  REDUCES CASUAL INTERRUPTIONS
- WITH SWIVEL CHAIR, YOU CAN
  LOOK OUT WHEN YOU WANT TO
- SECT'Y CAN BE IN LINE OF SIGHT
  THROUGH WINDOW

SHELVES FOR
REFERENCE BOOKS
& RECORDS

TIMER

PORTABLE
RECORDER

HANDS-FREE
TELEPHONE WITH
AUTOMATIC DIALER

CURRENT WORK &
READING ON SHELF

OUT IN

EASY ACCESS FOR
SECT'Y WHILE OTHERS
ARE IN THE OFFICE

COFFEE BAR

MEETING
ADAPTATION

BLACK-
BOARD

MOVEABLE
LAMP

SHELVES
OVER DESK

SHELVES OVER CABINET

WINDOW
TO SECT'Y